Renaissance and Medieval Studies

Edited by Charles Ross

Renaissance and Medieval Studies
Series Editor: Charles Ross, Purdue University

The Renaissance and Medieval Studies series focuses on editions, and translations of the Renaissance and earlier. The series also offers an outlet for electronic distribution of supplementary material for each printed volume from art history, film, and the history of the book. For more information, please visit the series Web page at parlorpress.com/pages/renaissance-and-medieval-studies or contact Parlor Press at editor@parlorpress.com.

Books in the Series

The Labyrinth of Love: Selected Sonnets and Other Poems by Pierre de Ronsard, Translated and Introduced by Henry Weinfield

Sir Philip Sidney's Arcadia. A Restoration in Contemporary English of the Complete 1593 Edition of *The Countess of Pembroke's Arcadia* by Charles Stanley Ross and Joel B. Davis, with an Essay on Musical Settings for the Poems by Edward Abe Plough (2017).

Sir Thomas Malory's Morte Darthur. A New Modern English Translation Based on the Winchester Manuscript by Dorsey Armstrong (2009).

Matteo Maria Boiardo's Orlando Innamorato. Translated with an Introduction and Notes by Charles Stanley Ross (2004).

PIERRE DE RONSARD

THE LABYRINTH OF LOVE

Selected Sonnets and Other Poems

Translated and Introduced by Henry Weinfield

Parlor Press
Anderson, South Carolina
www.parlorpress.com

Parlor Press LLC, Anderson, South Carolina, 29621

Translation by Henry Weinfield © 2021 by Parlor Press.
All rights reserved.
Printed in the United States of America.
S A N: 2 5 4 - 8 8 7 9

Library of Congress Cataloging-in-Publication Data

Names: Ronsard, Pierre de, 1524-1585, author. | Weinfield, Henry, translator. | Ronsard, Pierre de, 1524-1585. Poems. Selections. | Ronsard, Pierre de, 1524-1585. Poems. Selections. English.
Title: The labyrinth of love : selected sonnets and other poems / Pierre de Ronsard ; translated introduced by Henry Weinfield.
Description: Anderson, South Carolina : Parlor Press, [2021] | Series: Renaissance and medieval studies | Includes bibliographical references. | Summary: "Pierre de Ronsard is one of the greatest of all Renaissance lyric poets. This translation captures and conveys the intensity, passion, and musicality of his verse. An introduction, explanatory notes, and the French text are included"-- Provided by publisher.
Identifiers: LCCN 2021026603 (print) | LCCN 2021026604 (ebook) | ISBN 9781643172309 (paperback) | ISBN 9781643172316 (PDF) | ISBN 9781643172323 (EPUB)
Subjects: LCSH: Ronsard, Pierre de, 1524-1585--Translations into English. | LCGFT: Love poetry.
Classification: LCC PQ1675 .E5 2021 (print) | LCC PQ1675 (ebook) | DDC 841/.3--dc23
LC record available at https://lccn.loc.gov/2021026603
LC ebook record available at https://lccn.loc.gov/2021026604

978-1-64317-230-9 (paperback)
978-1-64317-231-6 (PDF)
978-1-64317-232-3 (EPUB)

Cover design by David Blakesley
Cover Image: "The Chariot of Apollo" by Odilon Redon. 1907. Oil on panel. The Fitzwilliam Museum, Cambridge UK. Used by permission
Printed on acid-free paper.

Parlor Press, LLC is an independent publisher of scholarly and trade titles in print and multimedia formats. This book is available in paperback and ebook formats from Parlor Press on the World Wide Web at http://www.parlorpress.com or through online and brick-and-mortar bookstores. For submission information or to find out about Parlor Press publications, write to Parlor Press, 3015 Brackenberry Drive, Anderson, South Carolina, 29621, or email editor@parlorpress.com.

Contents

Acknowledgments		*ix*
Introduction		*xiii*
	VOW	*3*
From *The Love Poems for Cassandra*		*5*
	I	*5*
	XI	*7*
	XX	*9*
	XXIII	*11*
	XXXI	*13*
	XXXII	*15*
	XXXVI	*17*
	XL	*19*
	XLIII	*21*
	XLIV	*23*
	L	*25*
	LII	*27*
	LVII	*29*
	LVIII	*31*
	LIX	*33*
	LXVIII	*35*
	LXXXI	*37*
	XCIV	*39*
	CIV	*41*
	CXIX	*43*
	CXX	*45*
	CXXIX	*47*
	CXXXV	*49*
	CXLV	*51*
	CLII	*53*
	CLX	*55*
	CLXV	*57*
	CLXXII	*59*
	CLXXIII	*61*
	CLXXIV	*63*
	CLXXX	*65*
	CXCII	*67*

CXCIII	69
CCXXVII	71
CCXXIX	73
From *The Love Poems for Marie*	**75**
II	75
IV	77
V	79
VI	81
IX	83
X	85
XIV	87
XIX	89
XXVIII	91
XXIX	93
XXXI	95
XLIV	97
LXIII	99
LXVI	101
LXVII	103
LXVIII	105
On the Death of Marie	**107**
I	107
II	109
III	111
IV	113
From *The First Book of Sonnets for Hélène*	**115**
III	115
VI	117
VII	119
IX	121
XXII	123
XXVI	125
XXVII	127
XXXIII	129
XXXVI	131
XXXVIII	133
XLIV	135
L	137
LIII	139
LX	141

From *The Second Book Of Sonnets For Hélène*		143
	I	143
	XXVI	145
	XLI	147
	XLII	149
	XLIII	151
	XLIX	153
	LXV	155
	LXXV	157
Elegy		159
Discourse on the Misery of These Times		165
Elegy to Philippe Desportes of Chartres		193
Last Verses		203
	I	203
	II	205
	III	207
	IV	209
	V	211
	VI	213
About the Translator		215

Acknowledgments

During the many years in which I have been involved in translating Ronsard, I have been aided and sustained by a number of friends, colleagues, and institutions.

I am grateful to the National Endowment for the Arts, which awarded me a fellowship in translation for 2018/2019 that enabled me to take time off from my teaching duties at the University of Notre Dame and bring this project close to fruition.

At an early stage of the project, the advice of JoAnn Della Neva of the Notre Dame French Department proved extremely helpful. Robert Goulding, a historian of science in my home department at Notre Dame, the Program of Liberal Studies, helped clarify for me the Renaissance attitude to the plenum as it emerges in Ronsard's Sonnet LXXXI to Cassandra. I'm very grateful to him, as I am also to my friend and colleague in the department, Steve Fallon, who was always willing to take time off from his labors on Milton to read and respond to my translations, and to David O'Connor of Notre Dame's Philosophy Department, who read my Introduction with the meticulous care and acuity he brings to bear on writers as diverse as Plato and Shelley. And I'm deeply grateful to Katy Schlegel of the Notre Dame Classics Department, with whom I collaborated a number of years ago on a translation of Hesiod: she read all of these translations as they emerged, and her appreciation and support sustained my confidence in the project.

Richard Goodkin of the University of Wisconsin French Department, whose writing on Mallarmé was a strong influence on my thinking a quarter of a century ago when I was working the great Symbolist poet, generously and warmly responded to my Introduction. The detailed criticism I received from my friend Richard Strier of the University of Chicago English Department, both on the Introduction and on my translation of Ronsard's lengthy "Discourse on the Misery of These Times," was bracing and extremely helpful. I am deeply grateful to him, as I am to my friends Norman Finkelstein and Stuart Liebman for their responses to the translations, and to my wife, Joyce Block, who, though not always the greatest fan of Ronsard's idealizations of women, was willing to suspend her irritation for the sake of her husband's immersion in Ronsard's poetry.

I am grateful to Charles Ross, the editor of Parlor Press's Renaissance and Medieval Series, both for his belief in the value of these translations and for his helpful comments on the Introduction. And I would like to thank Terence Cave, Emeritus Professor of French Literature at Oxford, for his extraordinary generosity and for his willingness to enter into discussions about the details of individual poems.

It is not customary for one translator to extend gratitude to another, but I would like to say that I am strongly indebted to Malcolm Quainton and Elizabeth Vinestock, whose superb prose translations of Ronsard were of enormous help to me. Verse-translation is a horse of a different color, but there should be no shame in acknowledging that one has been influenced and guided by the work of those who have gone before.

My greatest debt is to my friend and colleague in the Notre Dame French Department, Alain Toumayan. Whenever I had completed a draft of a particular translation, I would knock on his door in Decio Hall (both of us had offices on the third floor), and no matter how busy he was, he was always willing to respond, almost immediately, to my labors and queries. I came to rely on his philological skills, his deep knowledge of French literature, his excellent judgment, and his extraordinary kindness. My errors and failings are all my own, but I hope that these translations are in some way worthy of the attention he lavished on them.

*   *   *

Three of the translations from *Les Amours de Cassandre*, Sonnet XXXVI ("In the same way, Phoebus, you used to bewail"), Sonnet XLIV ("I'd gladly be Ixion on his wheel"), and Sonnet CLII ("Brown-eyed Moon, goddess whose coal-black horses"), were included in *Chicago Review*, 58:3/4 (2014), 294–96. Three of the translations from *Les Amours de Marie*, Sonnet IX ("Whoever wished to rearrange your name"), Sonnet XXVIII ("Are you so cruel as not to want to love"), and Sonnet XXIX ("I love the violet and the lovely rose"), were included in *The Poetry Porch* (2015). I am grateful to the editors of both of these journals.

Henry Weinfield
New York City
September 2020

Introduction

Pierre de Ronsard (1524–1585) has often been regarded as the greatest poet in French literature prior to the nineteenth century.[1] He was called "the prince of poets" in his own time and is one of the "big three" of French writers of the sixteenth century, the other two being Rabelais and Montaigne. He was the leader of the Pléiade Movement, which sought, by assimilating the classics and joining classical modes, genres, and procedures to the new Petrarchan and Neoplatonist spirit of the time, to renovate French poetry and, as Dante had earlier done for Italian, to make the vernacular capable of poetic greatness. Indeed, as Gilbert Highet asserts in *The Classical Tradition,* Ronsard was "the founder of elevated lyric poetry on classical models, not only for France but for all modern Europe."[2] As a love poet and the author of sonnet sequences, Ronsard follows in the wake of Petrarch, of course, but Highet's point is that Ronsard's immersion in Greek poetry, especially Pindar, had a decisive impact on the subsequent tradition.[3] Ronsard's work is remarkable for its scope, energy, and amplitude: it ranges over all of the poetic genres (ode, hymn, sonnet, elegy, satire, epic, discourse), and in the two-volume Bibliothèque de la Pléiade edition encompasses more than 2,000 pages. Equally remarkable—especially for a poet of such copiousness and variety—is the consistently high level of Ronsard's craftsmanship and the unvarying beauty of his phrasing. These characteristics are a reflection of Ronsard's extraordinary intelligence, inventiveness, and sincerity: he says what he thinks and is rarely if ever dull. During the seventeenth and eighteenth centuries, his work was sometimes disparaged (for example, by Boileau), but, all in all, his influence on subsequent French poetry has been enormous.

I approach Ronsard not primarily as a scholar but as a poet, one who, during the last ten years, has been immersed in Ronsard's

---

1. See Terence Cave, "Preface," *Ronsard the Poet,* ed. Terence Cave (London: Methuen and Co., 1973), 1.
2. Gilbert Highet, *The Classical Tradition: Greek and Roman Influences on Western Writing* (New York: Oxford UP, 1957), 233.
3. See *The Classical Tradition,* 230–35.

poetry and devoted to the project of rendering it into English verse. Verse translation, as I understand and practice it, is a paradoxical, not to say impossible, enterprise. In "bringing across" (the meaning of *translation*) another poet, my aim is simultaneously to get as close as possible to the original and to create a poem of my own. I want the original *en face*—placed side by side with the translation—for two antithetical reasons: first, because it is what the translation is trying to render, but, second, because it is what the translation must depart from in certain ways, and I want these departures to be transparent. At the same time, however, I want the translation to be a poem in its own right that has no need of the original and, in effect, is its own original. These two aims may strike the reader as logically incommensurate, but in practice the translation process involves a dialectical accommodation of one to the other. Whether or to what extent it succeeds in a given instance is of course another question.

There is a sonnet in Ronsard's first book of love poems, *Les Amours de Cassandre* (1552), that speaks to a crucial aspect of what he was trying to accomplish, especially at this early stage of his career, and at the same time to what is involved in the translation process. In the Pléiade edition (which will be my text throughout), it is number XXXVI in the sequence. I quote it in both the French and in my translation:

> Pour la douleur qu'Amour veut que je sente,
> Ainsi que moy Phebus tu lamentois,
> Quand amoureux et banny tu chantois
> Pres d'Ilion sur les rives de Xante.
>
> Pinçant en vain ta lyre blandissante,
> Fleuves et fleurs et bois tu enchantois,
> Non la beauté qu'en l'ame tu sentois,
> Qui te navroit d'une playe aigrissante.
>
> Là de ton teint tu pallissois les fleurs,
> Là les ruisseaux s'augmontoyent de tes pleurs,
> Là tu vivois d'une esperance vaine.

> Pour mesme nom Amour me fait douloir
> Pres de Vandôme au rivage du Loir,
> Comme un Phenis renaissant de ma peine.⁴
>
> In the same way, Phoebus, you used to bewail
> The sadness that Love now decrees that I feel,
> When lovesick and banished you sang on the shores
> Of the Xanthus, fair river near Ilion's towers.
>
> Plucking your blandishing lyre in vain,
> Streams, flowers, and woods you enchanted again
> And again, but the beauty that made your soul wounded
> Was not moved at all by the music you sounded.
>
> There, from your pallor, the flowers were made pale;
> There, from your tears would the rivulets swell;
> There, your vain hopes made you live in despair.
>
> Now Love makes me grieve for the very same name—
> Near the town of Vendôme on the shores of the Loir,
> Like a Phoenix reborn from my sorrow's own flame.

The two vectors of Ronsard's inspiration as a lyric poet are his relationship to experience and his relationship to literary tradition; they are beautifully blended in his work, and this is one index of its greatness. Sara Sturm-Maddox has argued that in the sonnet quoted above Ronsard may have been influenced by Petrarch, who had drawn on the story from Ovid's *Metamorphoses* in which Apollo laments the loss of the nymph Daphne;⁵ indeed, as we shall frequently see, the *Metamorphoses* is perhaps the single most important of all the classical influences that exerted themselves on Ronsard. But what the sonnet reveals, first and foremost, is how the circumstances of Ronsard's own experience opened up a rich vein of mythology

---

4. Pierre de Ronsard, *Œuvres complètes*, ed. Jean Céard, Daniel Ménager, and Michel Simonin (Paris: Gallimard, 1993), 1. 42-43. I shall sometimes refer to this edition simply as the Pléiade edition.

5. See Sara Sturm-Maddox, *Ronsard, Petrarch, and the Amours* (Gainesville, FL: University of Florida Press, 1999), 16.

that released his creative abilities. The young woman who inspired the sonnet was in fact named Cassandra. She was Cassandra Salviati, the daughter of a banker, and she was fifteen when Ronsard first met her. That she happened to be named Cassandra was, of course, an accident (unless Ronsard chose her for her name), but it had the effect of thrusting the poet into the story of Apollo and Cassandra that Ronsard would have found in the version recounted by Ovid in the *Heroïdes*. In the story (ultimately derived from Aeschylus's *Agamemnon*), Apollo promises the Trojan princess Cassandra the gift of prophecy if she will accede to his desires; she agrees, but after receiving the gift, she refuses the god, who, to punish her, decrees that her prophecies will never be believed. As Ronsard's sonnet makes clear, what interests him is not the story per se but rather the parallel that he is able to draw between Apollo as an unrequited lover and his own situation. Thus, just as Apollo, the god of poetry, sings on the shores of the Xanthus in Troy, so Ronsard, the modern poet, sings on the shores of the River Loir (not to be confused with the much larger Loire), which runs alongside his native town of Vendôme in central France. Now, what is accomplished by this parallel? What psychic work does it perform? The answer, I think, is that by establishing the parallel Ronsard appropriates the glory associated with the ancients in such a way as to transform his own "prosaic" reality into a "poetic" one. This gesture of appropriation—or, as we might say, of *translation*—is central to Renaissance classicism.

At the same time that Ronsard appropriates to himself the glory associated with Apollo, he conjures the figure of Orpheus, the archetypal poet who charmed the woods and streams, singing so beautifully that Nature resounded to his song. In Ronsard's conception, there is a correspondence between Apollo's grief and the response of Nature ("There, from your pallor, the flowers were made pale"). The Orphic conception that Ronsard develops underscores the poet's ambition to *enchant*—a word that brings together the ideas of music and magic. The poet's incantatory verse possesses a magical power to lift language beyond the prosaic immediacies of ordinary discourse. Here again, by imitating the god and assuming the Orphic quest, Ronsard takes on the mantle of poetry and releases his own creative powers.[6]

---

6. Mallarmé, who was deeply influenced by Ronsard, asserts in a letter to

I have chosen to highlight this sonnet because of the symbolic significance it bears to the translation process. Just as in writing the sonnet Ronsard attempts to appropriate a mythical glory or resonance, so in translating it I attempt to bring over into my own language, epoch, and idiom possibilities that would otherwise be unavailable.. It was perfectly natural for a Renaissance poet steeped in the classics and in the Neoplatonist thought of his time to invoke Apollo; for us, however, gestures of this kind are virtually impossible: the disenchantment of the world has gone too far in divesting poetry of its traditional symbolism, and, in the process, has rendered such gestures practically meaningless. Not that there is a point in lamenting the loss of tropes and poetic possibilities that are no longer relevant, but it is worth pointing out that like Ronsard's phoenix in the sonnet ("Like a phoenix reborn from my sorrow's own flame"), translation allows for a process of retrieval that can lead to cultural renewal. For that reason, it is vital to the handing down that goes by the name of tradition.

Verse-translation poses challenges and difficulties of various kinds, and here, taking Sonnet XXXVI from the Cassandra sequence as an example, I should like to address a few of the technical problems involved in translating Ronsard before passing on to other matters. First, French prosody is quantitative and thus substantially different from the English accentual-syllabic system: it is defined metrically by the number of syllables per line, but, unlike English prosody, its accents do not occur in a regular pattern; as a result, the two systems do not map onto each other in a symmetrical way. If Ronsard is writing in decasyllabics, as he is in *Les Amours de Cassandre*, this does not mean that a given sonnet will necessarily lend itself to iambic pentameter; by the same token, if, as in his other collections of love sonnets, he is working in alexandrines, the twelve-syllable line that increasingly became the metrical norm for French poetry after and to some extent because of Ronsard, an English hexameter line will not necessarily be effective. (Hexameters usually don't work in English because the caesura tends to fall directly in the

---

Verlaine of 1895 that the poet's "sole duty" is "the Orphic understanding of the earth." See Stéphane Mallarmé, *Selected Prose Poems, Essays, and Letters*, trans. Bradford Cook (Baltimore: The Johns Hopkins Press, 1956), 15.

middle of the line, after the third foot, and as a result they become monotonous.) While most of my translations of Ronsard's sonnets are in iambic pentameter, in the case of Sonnet XXXVI the translation spontaneously took the form of a four-beat (tetrameter) line in which anapestic feet are interspersed with iambic ones ("In the SAME / way PHOE / bus you USED / to beWAIL // The SAD / ness that LOVE / now deCREES / that I FEEL"). I have used a variety of meters and measures in these translations, including "fourteeners" (iambic heptameter couplets) and even "Poulter's Measure" (couplets in which iambic hexameter and iambic heptameter alternate). Moreover, though I am working in rhyme and meter, I do not attempt to replicate the rhyme scheme of the Petrarchan octave (abba abba). French, being a Romance language, is much richer in rhymes than English, and the attempt to keep the Petrarchan rhyme scheme in all cases would invariably lead to awkward, stilted writing. I make considerable use of slant rhyme (rhyme in which the consonantal ending is the same but the vowel is slightly changed). In striving for musicality, as I am doing, I sometimes need to omit unnecessary details (thus, in line 8, I do not translate the fact that the "playe" or wound is "aigrissante" or "festering"), and at other times I slightly embellish what is given (thus, lines 3 and 4, "tu chantois / Pres d'Ilion sur les rives de Xantes"—literally, "you sang near Ilion on the shores of the Xanthus"—becomes, slightly echoing Marlowe's "topless towers of Ilium," "you sang on the shores / Of the Xanthus, fair river near Ilion's towers"). My hope is that I manage to convey something of the music, the feeling-tone, and—in its most crucial details—the meaning of Ronsard's verse in a way that is faithful to his poetry while simultaneously expressing something of my own sensibility.

In the pages that follow, I shall comment on some of the dominant stylistic and thematic features of Ronsard's verse, first in the early Cassandra poems, then in the sonnets devoted successively to Marie and Hélène, then in the "Discourse on the Miseries of These Times" and the two elegies I have translated, and finally in the "Derniers Vers," the sonnets written on his death-bed with which my selection concludes. Except for the "Discourse" and the elegies, I have arranged my selection chronologically. I don't think we can say as a general rule that Ronsard's poetry increases in complexity because (as we have already begun to see) some of the Cassandra sonnets are themselves exceedingly complex. But as Ronsard's career develops, he continually takes on new engagements without jettisoning any of the old ones, and so his art both broadens and deepens over time.

The basic themes that charge the Cassandra sonnets are beauty, love, Nature, and the power of Eros—not as a set of separate concerns but as a continually changing constellation. These are the staples of love poetry, always and everywhere, but in addition to Ronsard's extraordinary mastery of the sonnet form, of metaphor, and of rhythm and cadence, his poetry is distinguished by its seriousness and sincerity. In Sonnet CXCIII, for example, in which he describes his beloved's breasts, sensuality and eroticism are combined with an idealism that is not merely conventional (and thus cannot merely be reduced to a Petrarchan trope) but rather the product of real commitment. Ronsard is neither a sensualist nor the kind of Neoplatonist for whom physical beauty is a stepping-stone to a higher spiritual beauty.[7] As Isidore Silver has demonstrated, the account of Eros in Ronsard has its underpinnings in Plato's *Symposium* and *Phaedrus*, where Eros is conjoined with the Good, as well as in Hesiod's *Theogony*, where Eros is one of the most ancient of the gods.[8] Ronsard is in continual dialogue with Plato throughout his career, and, in the radical hyperbole of this sonnet's concluding tercet, there is an insistence that the physical and spiritual are conjoined, that the spiritual is embodied in the physical and only has meaning because it can take a sensual form:

> These two twin streams of clotted milk that flow
> Over a valley white itself as snow—
> They are like tides approaching near the shore,
> Which slowly ebb and slowly flow back once more.

---

7. I would thus take issue with A. H. T. Levi, who writes: "From the beginning Ronsard's view of love is limited to its sensuous perspectives" ("The Role of Neoplatonism in Ronsard's Poetic Imagination," in *Ronsard the Poet*, 128).
8. Isidore Silver, *The Intellectual Evolution of Ronsard* (Saint Louis, MO: Washington UP, 1969), 1:165–214.

> A space between them forms, as if between
> Hills, where a leveled pathway can be seen,
> White from the drifts of snow with which it's filled—
> In winter, when the wind drops and is stilled.
>
> Two gleaming rubies there are raised on high:
> They lend their radiance to the ivory
> That smoothly curves around them on all sides.
>
> All honor there, and there all grace abides;
> And beauty, if the world has any, flies
> To the abode of this fair paradise.

What I find most moving in this sonnet is the clause "if the world has any" ("si quelqu'une est au monde"). It conveys a certain ironic skepticism about the world and about the Platonic realm of idealization that is an index of Ronsard's originality. From a certain perspective, the world is a place in which such ideals as honor, grace, and beauty are conspicuously absent; insofar as they exist, they float uselessly in some Platonic realm above and beyond human life and human interaction. But when desire is infused with love, these ideals can be materialized. There is nothing prurient or even particularly arousing in this sonnet: we are left with an impression of meditative stillness (hence the metaphorical stilling of the wind in the octave) and calm peacefulness.

I am pleased with the translation but fully aware of the fact that it does not capture the manner in which Ronsard's idea emerges from his rhyme in the concluding tercet:

> Là tout honneur, là toute grace abonde:
> Et la beauté, si quelqu'une est au monde,
> Vole au sejour de ce beau paradis.

Here, as always in Ronsard, thought in the abstract does not merely guide expression but also is guided and initiated by form and language.

Does Ronsard, in company with other love poets of the period, objectify women in his poetry? The issue is fraught in many ways, and of course the concept of objectification can be given various meanings. If to describe a woman's breasts is to objectify her, then certainly Ronsard is guilty as charged. If desire always involves objectification, then, yes, Ronsard is guilty, but so is the entire lyric tradition. But if to objectify means to relate to a woman as an *object*, and hence as the mere object of cold lust, then Ronsard is surely innocent. It is true that the woman of the sonnet is not so much a person in her own right as an embodiment of the eternal feminine—and one can therefore sympathize with those readers who view Ronsard's very idealizations as merely the obverse of the subjugation of women in this era. But perhaps our current cultural milieu has moved so far in the direction of cynicism that cynicism has become a cliché of its own, and perhaps we need the assistance of a poet such as Ronsard, now more than ever, to restore us to the possibility of idealization and to align it with our changed sense of reality. Now as always, this is the task of lyric poetry.

Sonnet XXIII ("This lovely coral, marble breathing sighs") is a poem that in many respects is similar to CXCIII in the concreteness of its physical description but is even more complex in the way it reaches for transcendence. Both begin with the figure of *deixis*, with the gesture of pointing, and with metaphorical elaborations on the woman's body: in Sonnet CXCIII, a winter landscape that gives way to gleaming rubies; in XXIII, gems and precious substances, with their brilliant colors, that evoke and are evoked by her body, in its parts and as a whole. The latter poem is addressed to Ronsard's friend and fellow member of the Pléiade, Rémy Belleau, who is noted for his poems on gems. In the sestet, referring to the metaphorical gems, metals, and flowers he has just catalogued and enumerated, Ronsard writes:

> They stir up in my soul such deep commotion
> That nothing can elicit an emotion
> Except their beauty, Belleau, which I adore;
>
> This and the pleasure that can never wane
> Of dreaming, thinking, thinking yet again,
> Dreaming and thinking, thinking yet once more.

What is extraordinary here is the way Ronsard penetrates and articulates an experience of beauty—not through metaphor, although after many metaphorical elaborations, but simply by repeating and giving rhythmic expression to the words "dreaming" and "thinking" ("songer, penser et repenser, / Songer, penser et repenser encore"). What he articulates, in other words, is both an experience of pure consciousness and that such an experience is impenetrable and transcends articulation.

I have been discussing poems in which the eroticism is somewhat idealized, but the Cassandra sequence contains many sonnets in which desire is expressed openly (one might almost say "nakedly") and with complete candor, though without the slightest coarseness or hypocrisy. One wonders how a poet who had received the tonsure in 1543 and was thus eligible for Church benefices, though he was never expected to perform as a priest, managed to free himself from Christian scruples quite so completely. The answer, I think, is two-fold: first, in the case of Cassandra, who was, after all, a married woman (the situation is quite different with Marie and Hélène), because there is not the slightest possibility that he will ever actually manage to get her into bed—here it is strictly a case of what the French call *amour de loin*; and second, and perhaps more importantly, because Ronsard's use of Greek mythology enables him to take on the lineaments of paganism.

Sonnet XX offers itself as a prime example:

> I wish I could turn to a rich, golden shower
> And rain drop by drop and hour by hour
> Into the lap of Cassandra, while sleep's
> Vapors seep into her eyes and she sleeps.
>
> Then I wish I could turn to a snowy-white bull
> And bear on my back one so beautiful
> That when she goes walking, a flower in spring,
> The flowers themselves find her ravishing.
>
> To ease my great burden of sorrow I dream
> Of being turned to Narcissus and she to a stream
> In which I can plunge and the whole night remain.

> Moreover, I wish that this night were forever
> And that the goddess Aurora would never
> Illumine the morning to wake me again.

Laced with Ovidian myths, this sonnet is a poem of pure wish-fulfillment. It is certainly not profound, but to me it expresses a charming sense of naïveté and innocence. It has just a touch of sadness, which derives from the hard lesson that life for us mortals isn't what it is for the gods. For Ronsard, who in many respects is an Epicurean, just as for Lucretius, the gods inhabit an idealized plane of existence against which our own diminished and tragic one can be measured.

Part of the Ovidian flavor of the Cassandra sequence has to do with the way in which Nature is aligned with the realm of the gods. In Sonnet CLX, as in Sonnet XX, only the poet experiences sadness and solitude, but the irony here is that these feelings are exacerbated by his awareness of the beauty and plenitude surrounding him:

> Now when great Jove in his virility
> Wants to engender his dear progeny,
> And from his burning loins spurts jets of spume,
> Inseminating Juno's hot, wet womb:
>
> Now when the sea, now when the winds so wild
> And vehement, to great armadas yield,
> Now when the bird amidst the forest's boughs
> Against the Thracian her complaint renews:
>
> Now when the meadows, when so many flowers,
> With thousands upon thousands upon thousands of colors,
> Are painting the bosom of the earth so gay,
>
> Among secluded rocks, sad and apart,
> I count my sorrows with a muffled heart:
> Hiding my wounds, through woods I make my way.

Structured around anaphoric repetitions of the word "Now" ("Or" in the French), the sonnet conveys an extraordinary feeling of vitality and immediacy. Human beings are not excluded: the armadas ("grans vaisseaux armez") opening their sails to the wind are as fully enveloped in *life*—for that, finally, is what is being described and praised—as the gods, the birds, and the flowers. The feeling of exclusion and deprivation that the poet expresses in the final tercet is merely contingent, a function of his own sadness and unrequited desire. There is only a hint of the awareness that we as a species are not enfolded in being and that this deficiency separates us both from the gods and from the rest of Nature.[9] Thus when Ronsard alludes in lines 7–8 to Ovid's tale of Philomela, we see the extent to which his landscapes, absorbed from Ovid, are also idealized.

One might go so far as to say that in poems such as these the artistic achievement has to do with the way Christianity has been *excluded* from the poet's frame of reference. Ronsard was not alone, of course, but how did he and his fellow artists and poets manage to find their way back not only to the classics but to a quasi-pagan vision of Nature? There are obvious answers (Neoplatonism, the recovery of an Epicurean outlook through the rediscovery of Lucretius), but to my mind there is still something deeply mysterious about this attempt on the part of Christian poets such as Ronsard to go beyond a Christian frame of reference.

That is certainly not how it would have been explained at the time, however. Consider the following passage from Ronsard's own "Abbregé de l'art poëtique" ("Summary of the Art of Poetry"), which he wrote in 1565. "Above all things," the poet insists,

> you will hold the Muses in reverence . . . for the daughters of Jupiter, which is to say, of God, who from his holy grace first made known through them to ignorant peoples the excellences of his majesty. For Poetry in the first age was naught but an allegorical Theology with the purpose of allowing into the minds of savage

---

9. Ronsard's sonnet might profitably be compared in this regard with a post-Enlightenment poem such as Wordsworth's Petrarchan sonnet "The world is too much with us." In the latter, the experience of a subject/object division motivates the poet to make artificial use of the personified gods of Greek mythology to return to what he frankly acknowledges is "a creed outworn." As Wordsworth clearly understands—and this is what makes his poem so great—the attempt to do this is no longer possible. For Ronsard, by contrast, in the sixteenth century, there is no sense that in adopting the lineaments of paganism he is embracing a creed outworn.

men through pleasing and shadowy fables the secrets that they were not able to understand when their truth was revealed too openly to them. . . . For the Muses, Apollo, Mercury, Pallas and other such deities represent to us nothing else than the powers of God, to which the first men had given many names [to represent] the diverse effects of his incomprehensible majesty.[10]

By suggesting that poetry in "the first age" was an allegorical theology, Ronsard is anticipating the ideas of Giambattista Vico, who in *The New Science* (1744) argued that Homeric religion is a "poetic theology" that should be seen on a continuum with and as leading to monotheism. But when, turning to the present, Ronsard asserts that the Muses and the gods "represent to us nothing more than the powers of God," he is also, I would suggest, defending himself against the possible charge that his own poetry is rife with paganism—a charge that was sometimes leveled specifically against Catholic writers by Protestant controversialists. Ronsard was a faithful and, indeed, at the time he wrote the "Abbregé," a militant Catholic, as we shall see,[11] but the passage strikes me as defensive and evasive. It is possible (though I think unlikely) that Ronsard thought that he was creating an allegorical theology, but it is obvious that what he was doing in much of his lyric poetry was something altogether different. The Jupiter of Sonnets XX and CLX (in the examples quoted above) can hardly be seen as a figure for God the Father in a monotheistic frame of reference. If one insists on holding onto the concept of allegorical theology in the case of Ronsard, one would have to say that in these poems it pertains to a religion quite different from Christianity.

Terence Cave suggests that for Ronsard, "the role of myth is the role of poetry itself: it evokes a magical world which is unreal and which nevertheless seems to comprehend truths fundamental to reality."[12] This observation is certainly true, and if we apply the concept of an "allegorical theology" to Ronsard's poetry in this sense, it would be an accurate description of his aims. Indeed, in Cave's

---

10. Ronsard, *Œuvres complètes*, 2.996; translation mine.

11. See the discussion below of Ronsard's "Discourse on the Misery of These Times."

12. Terence Cave, "Ronsard's Mythological Universe," in *Ronsard the Poet*, 207.

view, "there is little doubt that [the concept of an allegorical theology] acted as a catalyst for [Ronsard's] poetic imagination, and that without it his work would have been much less rich in significance." He adds: "Once the supernatural framework begins to fall away, poetry is left with no guarantee other than its own intrinsic power to create, to maintain the dialogue between reality and the imagination, and thus to compensate in some measure for the deficiencies and intractabilities of ordinary experience" (207). The "supernatural framework" that would have fallen away for Ronsard, however, was certainly not the Homeric religion but rather Judeo-Christian monotheism. There are thus two senses in which the term "allegorical theology" can be used with reference to Ronsard's poetry, one true and the other false. Insofar as the poet turns to the realm of mythology "to comprehend truths fundamental to reality," as Cave suggests, the term is accurate; but insofar as it is a response to the charge of paganism, it is an obfuscation.

Indeed, only rarely in the Cassandra poems do we get the intrusion of Judeo-Christian or biblical elements, and, when they occur, they are often melded with classical or mythological ones—as in Sonnet CXLV:

> My spirits were sunk in gloom and much I grieved
> When from my place of torment I received
> The golden fruit, grown yellow, as was I,
> From the same sickness that gives so much joy.
>
> The Apples are the gift that Love accords:
> O warlike Atalanta, this you know;
> And you, Cydippe, still have cause to rue
> How piercing were the letter's golden words.
>
> The Apples are Love's sign, and only he
> That's worthy of the apple can be blessed!
> Venus has always held them to her breast.
>
> Since Adam, our desire for it's the same.
> Each Grace has one in hand habitually,
> And Love, in brief, is just an apple game.

In this brilliant sonnet, Eros is simultaneously the source of joy and of pain, and the "Apples" (all of the metaphorical fruits that can be subsumed under that rubric) are its tangible sign and symbol ("le vray signe" in line 9 of the French). Apples are frequently compared to women's breasts in Ronsard's poetry,[13] so what is said of Venus in line 11 fits into a symbolic pattern or constellation. When Adam enters the picture at the end of the poem, his appearance is only tangentially from the standpoint of Original Sin; for in Ronsard's vision of Nature and human nature, there was never a pre-sexual state of innocence that was then succeeded by a state of sinfulness. "Since Adam" simply means "since human beings have existed."

The poem has a remarkable clarity that is typical of Ronsard, not only at this stage but throughout his career. If one follows the turnings of Ronsard's poems closely enough, their underlying meanings are always accessible. Line 10, "Heureux celuy qui de la pomme est digne!" ("Happy is he who is worthy of the apple"; in my version: "only he / That's worthy of the apple can be blessed!"), can serve as an example. In Ronsard's conception, there is no happiness that is not finally connected to Eros, and therefore, no happiness that is removed from pain and suffering: to have the capacity for happiness, to be *worthy* of the apple, is to be equal to this understanding and able to endure the sorrow that comes with joy. For that reason, the poem's final line, "Et bref l'Amour n'est qu'un beau jeu de pommes" ("And Love, in brief, is just an apple game"), is balanced between pessimism (with even a slight tinge of cynicism) and something like gaiety.

I have been suggesting that the poem is a kind of ode on melancholy. It is not impossible that Keats, who was strongly enamored of Ronsard's poetry, would have read and remembered it. The conclusion to his "Ode on Melancholy" presents a conception that is strangely similar:

> Ay, in the very temple of Delight
> Veil'd Melancholy has her Sovran shrine,
> Though seen of none save him whose strenuous tongue
> Can burst Joy's grape against his palate fine;

---

13. Another example is Sonnet LXVII of *Les Amours de Marie*, which I discuss below.

> His soul shall taste the sadness of her might,
> And be among her cloudy trophies hung.[14]

The poems in the *Continuation des Amours, Les Amours de Marie* (1555) have a different tonality from those in the Cassandra sequence, partly because the two women were very different. Marie (surnamed Dupin or Du Pin) was from the countryside of Anjou and for that reason the sonnets addressed to her tend to have a more pastoral flavor and seemingly a greater simplicity than those for Cassandra: they are steeped in Nature and the pleasures of the countryside, and the mythological scaffolding surrounding them tends to be less elaborate and pronounced. Quite a few of them are simple invitations to partake of the pleasures of love. Where Cassandra's name had led the poet back to Homer and Aeschylus, Marie's, he tells us, is simply an anagram for the French verb:

> Whoever wished to rearrange your name
> Would find *aimer*: so love me, then, Marie.
> Love calls you by your name—it's Nature's *aim*.
> Traitors to Nature get no clemency.
>
> Marie, qui voudroit vostre nom retourner,
> Il trouveroit aimer: aimez-moy donc Marie,
> Vostre nom de nature à l'amour vous convie.
> A qui trahist Nature il ne faut pardonner.

In addition to the oft-repeated invitations and proposals, the poems to Marie contain rebukes because of her reluctance to take him up on them. Sonnet XXVIII is an example:

> Are you so cruel as not to want to love?
> Is it contempt for Nature? See the sparrow:
> The urge to love has stirred him to the marrow;
> Behold the ringdove and the turtledove.
>
> See how the amorous birds on quivering wing
> Are fluttering here and there from bough to bough:

---

14. *Selected Poems and Letters by John Keats*, ed. Douglas Bush (Boston: Houghton Mifflin, 1959, lines 25–30.

> The young vine curls around the elm trees now:
> All things are filled with laughter in the spring.
>
> The shepherdess, turning her spindle, sings
> Her loves; the shepherd tunes his melody
> To answer her; for love is in all things.
>
> All speak of love, all enter in its fire:
> Only your heart, as cold as it can be,
> Stays obstinate and still disdains desire.

There is a lightness of touch to many of these poems, but the mood darkens when death makes itself felt as a reality. I want to examine two of the Marie sonnets—the first not particularly well known, the second, from the concluding section entitled "On the Death of Marie," among the most famous in French literature—in both of which Ronsard invokes the rose, the quintessential symbol of beauty in the Western world, against the possibility and reality of death.

In Sonnet LXVII, Marie is figured as a "Goddess" (a word always capitalized in Ronsard's lexicon) whose transcendent beauty is beyond the reach of praise and not subject to change. She is "[t]he flower of flowers, the quintessential rose" ("La fleur des fleurs la rose de la rose"). The bouquet that the poet *composes* ("For you, in vain, this garland I compose") is both a garland of actual flowers and, metaphorically, the gathering together of his verses—including this very poem. The sestet is framed as an invocation to the roses that form the bouquet.[15] But as it reveals, if the actual flowers were to come into contact with her transcendent beauty, they would fade:

> Happy bouquet, you should not ever come
> To this fair breast, where Love has made its home,
> Or touch the twin ripe apples that are there.
>
> Your brilliant luster would soon fade away,
> Your freshness wither, subject to decay,

---

15. I am reminded of Edmund Waller's lyric, "Go, lovely rose" (1645), which also invokes the rose and which might possibly have been influenced by Ronsard.

As I have withered out of love for her.

By contrast, in "Comme on voit sur la branche au mois de May la rose," the fourth sonnet in "On the Death of Marie," the terms are reversed; for here the rose's beauty is intensified by the reality of death. Apparently, the poems under this heading were included only in 1578 and were composed in memory of a different Marie: Marie de Clèves, the wife of Henri de Bourbon, the prince of Condé.[16] It seems to me likely that Ronsard's feelings about the young woman from Anjou influenced these later poems; but what is important for us as readers, in any event, is not the circumstances surrounding the poem's composition but the poem itself:

> Just as one sees the rose on its stem in May,
> In youthful beauty, in its earliest flower,
> Making sky jealous of its vibrant color,
> By Dawn's tears watered at the break of day:
>
> Grace in each fold and love in full display,
> Embalming the gardens and the trees with odor;
> But beaten by rain or by excessive ardor,
> Languish and die, till fold upon fold falls away:
>
> So in the earliest newness of your youth,
> Your beauty honored both by heaven and earth,
> Fate cut you off, and now your dust reposes.
>
> For obsequy, receive from me these tears,
> This bowl of milk, this basket full of flowers,
> So that alive and dead you are naught but roses

Two details in this great and justly famous poem deserve to be singled out and mentioned. The first is that the rose's beauty is "honored both by heaven and earth"—not, I think, because it transcends change and death but precisely because it is subject to them—and in this respect it is significant that heaven and earth ("la terre et le ciel") are both opposed by Fate ("La Parque"). The second is that the rose is "watered at the break of day" by "Dawn's tears" ("Quand

---

16. See *Œuvres complètes*, 1.1326.

l'Aube de ses pleurs au poinct du jour l'arrose"), a prolepsis that brings together the nurturing of the rose with the awareness of the short duration of its life and beauty. Translation, alas, is unable to capture the magnificent homonymic rhymes, "la rose" and "l'arrose" ("waters it") in lines 1 and 4.

The poems in the two books of *Sonnets pour Hélène* were written considerably later than those for Cassandra and Marie, probably between 1569 and 1578,[17] and were addressed to a lady of the court, Hélène de Surgères. Judging from the poems themselves, she seems to have been pious and something of an intellectual. Ronsard frequently discusses Plato with her, usually adopting a position opposed to Plato's body/soul dualism (for his own far from disinterested reasons) but sometimes agreeing with her and taking her part. As was the case with Cassandra, Ronsard makes much of Hélène's name, punning on it ("haleine" means "breath") and using it to robe himself in the mantle of the Homeric epics:

> Sweet Helen, breath of life, my sweet *haleine*,
> Warming my heart through your reviving chill,
> I draw from your strength and knowledge and remain
> Drawn by the eyes that lead me where they will.
>
> Happy is he who suffers a lover's pain
> For a name so fatal; happy is his ordeal:
> Blessèd the grief of one whose hope is still
> To gain not just the eyes but the star of Hélène.
>
> Name, bane of the Trojans, subject of my woe,
> My sage Penelope and my Helen too,
> Enveloping me in love's anxiety:
>
> Name, which has elevated me to heaven,
> Who would have ever thought that I'd be given
> In the same Helen a Penelope?

---

17. See Donald Stone, *Ronsard's Sonnet Cycles: A Study in Tone and Vision* (New Haven and London: Yale UP, 1966), 134; see also *Œuvres complètes*, 1.1356-57.

Ronsard is older now, and these are the poems of an aging lover who, particularly at the end of the sequence, feels himself defeated by time and change—as in Sonnet LXXV of the second book:

> I flee from the battle, my troops in defeat,
> For Love has deprived me of strength and of reason.
> I'm five decades old—my gray hairs commit treason:
> They're calling me home as they sound the retreat.
>
> If your glorification is not yet complete,
> Do not blame the spirit, blame only the season.
> I am neither Paris nor disloyal Jason:
> I'm obeying the law that Nature has set.
>
> Between the hope and the fear, the sweet and the bitter,
> Love polished this work in my forge. My lament
> Is not for the toil nor the time that I've spent.
>
> My lament's for myself and the falsehoods you utter.
> If you are kind-hearted, you will repent.
> But a tardy repentance will not make things better.

In this sonnet, the poet is finally *hors de combat*, as the French say; but here we have to make a crucial distinction. It is quite true, as Grahame Castor emphasizes, that the Hélène poems are more realistic and less given to idealization and hyperbole than those dedicated to Cassandra,[18] but if Ronsard refers to himself as *defeated* in the poem quoted above, this is as a lover, certainly not as a poet. "Love polished this work in my forge," he writes, with complete confidence that his work will be lasting. What he does not say—for that would indeed be a kind of "treason"—is that Love was perhaps a means to an end, not the end itself. The end, of course, was poetry.

The first poem by Ronsard that I translated and the one that first drew me to him, was "Quand vous serez bien vieille, au soir, à la chandelle," Sonnet XLIII from the second book of the *Sonnets pour Hélène*, one of the most famous poems in French literature. I had

---

18. See Grahame Castor, "Petrarchism and the Quest for Beauty in the *Amours* of Cassandre and the *Sonets pour Helene*," in *Ronsard the Poet*, especially 118–19.

encountered it originally through Yeats's imitation, "When You Are Old," which he included in his second collection of poems, *The Rose* (1893).[19] My translation, more freely rendered than most of the others I have since done, is in "Poulter's Measure":

> Some evening when you're old—the light begins to wane;
> You're spinning thread beside the fire and winding off the skein;
> Suddenly you recall the lines I spun and sung:
> "I was the inspiration for Ronsard when I was young."
>
> You'll be without a servant, who hears what you have said
> And, drowsy from her labor, only yearns to be in bed,
> But at the sound of Ronsard, risen, will not raise
> Blessings upon your very name with immortal praise.
>
> I'll be beneath the earth, a phantom without bones,
> A shade who's gone to take his rest where myrtles cast their shade;
> You'll be at the hearth, like other withered crones,
>
> Thinking upon my love and on your proud disdain with sorrow.
> If you believe me, live! Don't wait until tomorrow:
> Gather the roses life holds out before they start to fade.

Ronsard's sonnet concludes with the *Carpe diem* injunction, but what it actually envisions is a possibility in which no seizing of the day will have occurred. The poet imagines Hélène as an old lady spinning thread by candlelight in the future. (The trope of the woman spinning or weaving as a metaphor for poetry goes back to Homer: indeed, Helen in the *Iliad* is weaving the narrative of the Trojan War.). Remembering Ronsard's poems and reciting them to herself, filled with wonder, Hélène is imagined as saying, "Ronsard me celebroit du temps que j'estois belle" (literally: "Ronsard celebrated me in the time when I was beautiful"). What the poet imagines her saying in the future is, of course, the line of poetry that he is composing in the present; and thus, not only is there a strange collapsing of temporalities but a sense in which the still living poet turns into a phantom—one marked by his name. In the second quatrain, one of Hélène's servants, drowsy from her day's labor, is imagined as waking up to the sound of the

---

19. Yeats was deeply influenced by Ronsard. "Leda and the Swan," one of his only sonnets, may have been influenced by Ronsard's ode, "La Defloration de Lede."

poet's name—the name Hélène has just spoken—and blessing *her* name with "immortal praise"—that is, with the immortal praise the poet has conferred on her in this very poem. (The French employs a double negative here, thereby hinting at the absence / presence dialectic that is intrinsic to the poem's mysteriousness and beauty. Actually, in the strange syntax of the quatrain, there is not one of her servants who, hearing the name of Ronsard, who will not bless her.) In the sestet, the poet imagines Hélène as a withered crone at the hearth and himself as "a phantom without bones, / A shade . . . among the myrtle shades" (by doubling the word "shade," I make Ronsard's implicit pun explicit); that is, he imagines himself as nothing more than his poetry—indeed, the very poem that he is now in the act of composing!

Contemporary feminist readings of the sonnet complain that while Hélène—and thus women in general—belong to the world of immanence and mortality, the poet figures himself as transcendent and immortal. The complaint is to some extent justified. If we take the trope of the woman weaving as a figure for poetry, however, the sonnet ceases to be as narcissistic (or as dichotomizing) as it might initially appear. From this perspective, in addition to voicing the poem, Hélène, having provided the poet with the sonnet's metaphorical threads, joins with him in its composition.

By the time Ronsard came to compose the sonnets to Hélène—certainly the ones in the second book, in any event—he had largely withdrawn from the affairs of the court: in Sonnet XLI he refers to the court as "the Egyptian land . . . this land of slavery." During the 1560s, however, a time in which France was increasingly consumed by civil strife between its Catholics and Protestants, Ronsard was deeply embroiled in politics and employed in writing diatribes against the Protestant adversary. I have translated and included in this selection Ronsard's "Discourse on the Misery of These Times" (actually, the second section of this poem, usually referred to as the *Continuation du Discours des Miseres de ce temps*), a poem of more than 400 lines of alexandrine couplets that was composed in 1562. It was dedicated to Catherine de Medici (or Médicis), the queen mother, who was then regent of France—the same Catherine de Medici who, though initially connected with the party of moderation and reconciliation, would later be implicated (though some recent historians have begun to cast doubt on the extent to which she was responsible) in the Saint Bartholomew's Day Massacre of the Huguenots (French Calvinists) of 1572. Ronsard could not have known, of course, where things would lead, but he cannot be fully exonerated because, in a small way, his poetry may have prepared some of the ground for the violence to come. In his "Discourse on the Misery of These Times," he actually compares the Protestants to caterpillars that, if not eradicated, will soon take over a field and devour its crops. "Thus, while my Kings in foreign wars were vying," laments the personified figure of France, "These caterpillars went on multiplying, / So that in three months' time a frenzied crop / Had swarmed all over me and eaten me up." From our vantage point, that Ronsard should have played a partisan role in these sad polemics is of course deplorable, though at the same time readily understandable. He had very little interest in doctrinal matters—in my view, he was fundamentally an Epicurean in his outlook—but at the same time he felt that the Calvinists were responsible for the civil strife tearing up France and that, given their iconoclastic attitudes, they were bent on destroying the beautiful old religion and culture of which he himself was a part. The poem is rhetorically powerful and in certain passages beautiful. After all, it was written by Ronsard.

In addition to the "Discourse," I have included two elegies, both originally in alexandrine couplets but very different from each other. The one beginning "Six years had run," published for the first time in the 1584 edition of Ronsard's poetry, is addressed to Hélène and placed near the end of the second book of the sonnets to her.[20] It gives us an intimate picture, quite different from what we get in the sonnets, of Ronsard's relationship both to books and to Nature. The astrological passage in the middle of the poem that begins "When the evening star" strikes me as extraordinarily vivid and beautiful.

The elegy addressed to the court poet Philippe Desportes (1546–1606) and posthumously published in 1587 is unusual in that it is the only poem Ronsard ever annotated. I have rendered it in "fourteeners" (iambic heptameter couplets) to capture its gravity and the seriousness of its tone. The philosophical and religious views it espouses are strongly influenced by Aristotle—for whom the soul is the life of the body and therefore mortal—as well as by Lucretius.

---

20. See *Œuvres complètes*, 1.420–22.

In my own view, the poem's tone owes a good deal as well to the Old Testament Book of Ecclesiastes.

The annotations amount to a retraction of the views expressed in the poem; but given how much at odds those views are with the dominant religious thought of the time, whether Catholic or Protestant, this should not be surprising. The poet writes: "The dead aren't happy, as in them the soul that is perforce / The principle of movement has no longer any force." The annotator comments: "This is the opinion of Aristotle, which is false: for the dead that die in Christ are perfectly happy." It is true that this is Aristotle's view, but Ronsard is here attempting to distance himself from a statement that he clearly frames as his own in the poem. Again, the poet writes: "Nor should he [each person] feed on expectations of an eternity / Which isn't anything at all but smoke and vanity." To which the annotator responds: "Against the Poets, who promise themselves and others nothing less than eternity through their verses." It is true that the elegy, unusually for Ronsard, distances itself from the notion that poetry acquires a kind of immortality, but in this passage the poet addresses the idea of eternity per se, not specifically a poetic eternity. In their notes to the poem, Malcolm Quainton and Elizabeth Vinestock write: "The poem's disenchanted tone, its ambiguities and its deviation from Ronsard's frequent assertions of poetic immortality in favor of an epicurean attitude to fame, are all best read as a defensive, even ironical, commentary on the youthful Desportes's increasing popularity at court and in the literary salons from the mid-1570s onwards."[21] I disagree. It is the annotations that are defensive, not the poem. Ronsard may have been envious of Desportes, but what he asserts in the poem is, as always, what he happens to believe at the moment. That he felt compelled to add annotations to the poem, along with the fact that it was published posthumously, suggests that he may have worried that what the poem had to say would have been viewed by others as tantamount to atheism. Or he may have felt that he had gone too far and that the poem was in conflict with his own sentiments. Human beings are capable of holding diametrically opposed views. If "[a] foolish consistency is the hobgoblin of little

---

21. Pierre de Ronsard, *Selected Poems*, trans. Malcolm Quainton and Elizabeth Vinestock (New York: Penguin Books, 2002), 288.

minds," as Emerson said, this is one accusation that need not be leveled against Ronsard.[22]

The sonnets grouped under the heading "Last Poems" (*Derniers Vers*) are astonishing productions. The poet was dying when he wrote them, and, as he chronicles, unable to sleep and much of the time in great discomfort. Yet, as usual, we have these gorgeously controlled Petrarchan structures. Indeed, it seems almost as if Ronsard's experience of suffering increased his enjoyment of the process of poetic creation. There is something mordantly comic—Beckettian, perhaps—in his vision of himself as a skeleton as well as in his assertion that neither Apollo nor Asclepius would be able to cure him:

> I look like a skeleton stretched on a bier
> Without muscles or sinews—I'm nothing but bone
> That the arrow of death without mercy struck down.
> I can't look at my arms without trembling with fear.
>
> Apollo and his son, great doctors without peer,
> Wouldn't know how to cure me—their craft's come undone.
> My eyes have grown dim—farewell, cheerful sun,
> My body's going down where all things disappear.

One is reminded of Donne, wrapping himself up in a shroud for a final portrait of himself.

The sixth and last of the "Last Poems" is a great poem and has had a significant afterlife. Its traces lead directly to Mallarmé's "Swan" sonnet ("Le vierge, le vivace et le bel aujourd'hui"), and hence to the Symbolist Movement and modernity:

> Our dwellings and our orchards and our gardens we must leave,
> The vessels and the vases that our artisans engrave,
> And chant our funeral dirges, as the Swan with his last breath
> Does upon Maeander's shores to celebrate his death.

---

22. Ralph Waldo Emerson, "Self-Reliance," *The Portable Emerson*, ed. Carl Bode and Malcolm Cowley (New York: Penguin Books, 1981), 145.

> I have unwound my destiny's allotted thread—it's done.
> I've made my name significant: I've lived and I am known.
> My pen flies upward to the sky, there to become a sign—
> Far from the worldly snares to which even the wise incline.
>
> Happy is he who never was; more happy, who returns
> Back to the void from whence he came; more happy who sojourns
> With Jesus Christ, an angel now, though human formerly,
>
> Leaving to putrefy on earth his cast-off body's clay
> (With which fate, hazard, destiny, fortune, and chance all play)
> To be pure spirit—from the body's heavy chains set free.

In semiotic terms, the sonnet is built upon two irreducible features of the French language that translation is therefore unable to capture: first, the fact that "Cygne" and "signe" are homophones, and, second, that the word "plume" can mean both "pen" and "feather." In taking leave of his life, the poet compares himself to the swan, which is reputed to sing when it is about to die. The poet's pen (a metonymy for poetry), which "flies upward to the sky" ("Ma plume vole au Ciel"), is at the same time the feather of the swan. The "signe" is phonically, therefore, the "Cygne," which is to say, the constellation Cygnus, and this in turn means that the concept of eternity is symbolically juxtaposed against (and imposed upon) that of death. The fact that "ciel" can mean both "heaven" and "sky" allows for the possibility of both a secular and a religious interpretation of the ascent. It is the density of these figures, as well as the way they construct an allegory rooted in language, that is so modern and so Mallarméan.

A few other details in the sonnet are worth noting. In the opening line of the second quatrain, "C'est fait, j'ai devidé le cours de mes destins," Ronsard alludes to the Greek idea of fate or destiny, according to which the three *Moirai*—Clotho, Lachesis, and Atropos—were said to spin, measure, and cut the thread of human lives. In the ancient Greek conception, human beings are completely passive—acted upon rather than acting. The poet's language is ambiguous, however, and the line can be read both passively and actively: in one sense, his grammar acknowledges that he too is fated, but, in another, it suggests that, having created a life-work that is now complete ("C'est fait"), he has taken his destiny into his own hands and brought it to fulfillment.

In the three assertions in the sestet that are linked by the anaphoric repetition of "Happy," there is another set of interesting ambiguities. In the first ("Happy is he who never lived"), we have the pessimism of the ancients. ("Never to have lived is best," says the Chorus of Sophocles's *Oedipus at Colonus* in Yeats's translation.)[23] In the second ("more happy who returns / Back to the void from whence he came), the idea of nothingness or the void, recalling Hesiod's claim in the *Theogony* that the first of things was *Chaos* (i.e. Chasm), is added to this ancient pessimism. But in the third ("more happy who sojourns / With Jesus Christ"), and in the lines concluding the poem, there is the resurgence of a Christian vision built upon Platonic dualism. At the end of his life, apparently, all three of these possibilities existed simultaneously and without contradicting one another for the poet Ronsard.

---

23. See W. B. Yeats, "From 'Oedipus at Colonus,'" *Collected Poems* (New York: Macmillan, 1967), 223.

The Labyrinth of Love

VŒU

Divines Sœurs, qui sur les rives molles
De Castalie, et sur le mont Natal,
Et sur le bord du chevalin crystal
M'avez d'enfance instruit en vos escoles:

Si tout ravy des saults de vos caroles,
D'un pied nombreux j'ay guidé vostre bal,
Plus dur qu'en fer, qu'en cuivre et qu'en metal,
Dans vostre Temple engravez ces paroles:

Ronsard, afin que le siecle avenir
De temps en temps se puisse souvenir
Que sa jeunesse à l'amour fist homage,

De la main dextre apand à vostre autel
L'humble present de son livre immortel
Son cœur de l'autre aux pieds de ceste image.

VOW

Divine Sisters, who at the Castalian fount
Or on great Helicon, your natal mount,
Or on the crystal Hippocrene's sweet shores
Have been my teachers in that school of yours:

If ravished by the leaps of your choral song,
I've steered your dance with numerous feet (more strong
Than iron, copper, or than any metal),
Engrave these words in your illustrious Temple:

Ronsard, so he can shape a memory
Withstanding time for the coming century,
Of how his youth once rendered love due homage,

Unto your altar brings with his right hand
His deathless book, a humble present, and
His heart with the other at the feet of this image.[1]

---

1. Ronsard's "Vow" was intended as a preface to his entire book. The "image" to which he refers in line 14 is a drawing of the poet on the frontispiece of the volume that was intended to follow the "Vow."

1-4: In this invocation of the Muses, Ronsard mentions the Castalian Spring, where visitors to Delphi slaked their thirst, and the "chevalin crystal," the crystal spring of the Horse—which is to say, the Hippocrene. The waters of both the Castalian Spring and the Hippocrene were seen by the ancient Greeks as having the power to inspire poets. By "le mont Natal" ("natal mount"), Ronsard is referring by implication to Mount Helicon. Hence my translation, though this home of the Muses is not actually mentioned by name in the French text.

5-6: The dancing feet of the Muses are likened to the "numerous [metrical] feet" of the poet's verses. Just as in English, "numbers" can refer to verses (during the Renaissance and up to the eighteenth century), so too in French.

Les Amours de Cassandre,
Le Premier Livre des Amours

I

Qui voudra voir comme Amour me surmonte,
Comme il m'assaut, comme il se fait vainqueur,
Comme il r'enflame et r'englace mon cueur,
Comme il reçoit un honneur de ma honte:

Qui voudra voir une jeunesse pronte
A suivre en vain l'objet de son malheur,
Me vienne lire: il voirra la douleur,
Dont ma Deesse et mon Dieu ne font conte.

Il cognoistra qu'Amour est sans raison,
Un doux abus, une belle prison,
Un vain espoir qui de vent nous vient paistre:

Et cognoistra que l'homme se deçoit,
Quand plein d'erreur un aveugle il reçoit
Pour sa conduire, un enfant pour son maistre.

From *The Love Poems for Cassandra*

I

Whoever wants to see what Love can be,
How it assaults, subdues, and conquers me,
Freezing my heart and making it once more flame,
And how it reaps great honor from my shame:

Whoever wants to see a youth in vain
Pursuit of what can only cause it pain,
Should read my book: he'll learn of sorrow there—
Of which my God and Goddess take no care.

He'll come to know that Love is without reason,
A sweet deception, a fine-seeming prison,
A hope that on the wind would make us feed:

And he will know that that man is deceived,
Who, like a wandering blind man, has received
An infant as his master and his guide.[2]

---

2. Line 1: Here as elsewhere, Love is personified as a god, but also conceived as a power, an emotion, and a principle. The pronoun "il" in French can be both personal and impersonal, but the English translator has to choose.

5: Because the phrase "une jeunesse" contains an article, I have translated it as "a youth," but the meaning could also be "youth" in general.

8: Following the orthographical convention of his time, Ronsard almost always capitalizes the words "dieu" and "deesse," and so here and elsewhere I follow his lead. But what might be seen as blasphemous to our culture has no such connotations to his. Here the God is the "Amour" of line 1 (Ronsard sometimes uses the Latin form, Amor, but never the Greek, Eros) and the Goddess is Cassandra herself.

13-14: The blind infant is of course the god of love itself (Amor or Cupid).

XI

Ah traistre Amour, donne moy paix ou tréve,
Ou choisissant un autre trait plus fort,
Tranche ma vie, et m'avance la mort:
Douce est la mort d'autant plus qu'elle est bréve.

Un soing fecond en mon penser s'eleve,
Qui mon sang hume, et l'esprit me remord,
Et d'Ixion me fait egal au sort,
De qui jamais la peine ne s'acheve.

Que doy-je faire? Amour me fait errer
Si hautement, que je n'ose esperer
De mon salut qu'une langueur extréme.

Puis que mon Dieu ne me veut secourir,
Pour me sauver il me plaist de mourir,
Et de tuer la mort par la mort mesme.

XI

Ah, treacherous Love, accord me some relief,
Or choosing another arrow, with more power,
Cut off my life, hasten my final hour;
For death is sweet, so long as its throes are brief.

Prolific cares within my thought are rife—
They suck my blood and gnaw me to the core,
Making me like Ixion, past all cure,
Fated to endless suffering and grief.

What should I do? Love makes me go astray
So flagrantly I dare not even pray
For more than the extremest apathy.

Because my God no longer succors me,
To save myself my wish is but to die—
Through death itself to kill death instantly.[3]

---

3. Line 7: For the crime of lusting after Hera, Ixion (always pronounced IksEYEon in this translation) was tricked by Zeus into making love to a cloud, from which was born the founder of the race of centaurs. Ixion was then bound by Zeus to a fiery wheel. Ronsard makes frequent reference to the myth.

11: I have rendered "langueur extréme" in the French as "extremest apathy" because I think Ronsard is alluding to the Stoic doctrine of *apatheia*, a state in which one is not disturbed by the passions.

XX

Je voudroy bien richement jaunissant
En pluye d'or goute à goute descendre
Dans le giron de ma belle Cassandre,
Lors qu'en ses yeux le somne va glissant.

Puis je voudroy en toreau blanchissant
Me transformer pour sur mon dos la prendre,
Quand en Avril par l'herbe la plus tendre
Elle va fleur mille fleurs ravissant.

Je voudroy bien pour alleger ma peine,
Estre un Narcisse et elle une fontaine,
Pour m'y plonger une nuict à sejour:

Et si voudroy que ceste nuict encore
Fust eternelle, et que jamais l'Aurore
Pour m'esveiller ne rallumast le jour.

XX

I wish I could turn to a rich, golden shower
And rain drop by drop and hour by hour
Into the lap of Cassandra, while sleep's
Vapors seep into her eyes and she sleeps.

Then I wish I could turn to a snowy-white bull
And bear on my back one so beautiful
That when she goes walking, a flower in spring,
The flowers themselves find her ravishing.

To ease my great burden of sorrow I dream
Of being turned to Narcissus and she to a stream
In which I can plunge and the whole night remain.

Moreover, I wish that this night were forever
And that the goddess Aurora would never
Illumine the morning to wake me again.[4]

---

4. This freehand translation is in anapestic tetrameter. The phrases "hour by hour" in line 2 and "one so beautiful" in line 6 are my interpolations.

1-4: Zeus impregnated Danaë by coming to her in the form of a golden shower.

5-8: Zeus, in the form of a bull, abducted Europa, after whom the continent of Europe is named.

10-11: Narcissus fell in love with his own reflection in a pool of water.

13: Aurora, the goddess of the dawn, is frequently mentioned in Ronsard's poetry.

XXIII

Ce beau coral, ce marbre qui soupire
Et cet ebene ornement du sourci,
Et cet albâtre en voûte racourci,
Et ces saphirs, ce jaspe et ce porphyre:

Ces diamans, ces rubis, qu'un Zephyre
Tient animez d'un soupir adouci,
Et ces œillets et ces roses aussi,
Et ce fin or, où l'or mesme se mire:

Me sont dans l'ame en si profond esmoy,
Qu'un autre objet ne se presente à moy,
Sinon, Belleau, leur beauté que j'honore,

Et le plaisir qui ne se peut passer
De les songer, penser et repenser,
Songer, penser et repenser encore.

XXIII

This lovely coral, marble breathing sighs,
This ebony, adornment of the eyes,
This alabaster in its close-drawn vault,
Sapphires and porphyry, jasper without fault:

These diamonds and rubies that a breeze
Quickens to life with its soft breath, and these
Roses and carnations, this fine gold
Where gold itself discovers its own mold:

They stir up in my soul such deep commotion
That nothing can elicit an emotion
Except their beauty, Belleau, which I adore;

This and the pleasure that can never wane
Of dreaming, thinking, thinking yet again,
Dreaming and thinking, thinking yet once more.[5]

---

5. The poem is addressed to Rémy Belleau (1528-77), Ronsard's friend and a fellow member of the Pléiade movement. As Belleau is known for his poems about gems and precious stones, Ronsard's reference to him here is especially appropriate.

XXXI

Legers Démons qui tenez de la terre,
Et du haut ciel justement le milieu:
Postes de l'air, divins postes de Dieu,
Qui ses segrets nous apportez grand erre:

Dites Courriers (ainsi ne vous enserre
Quelque sorcier dans un cerne de feu)
Razant nos champs, dites, a'vous point veu
Cette beauté qui tant me fait la guerre?

Si de fortune elle vous voit çà bas,
Libre par l'air vous ne refuirez pas,
Tant doucement sa douce force abuse:

Ou comme moy esclave vous fera
De sa beauté, qui vous transformera
D'un seul regard, ainsi qu'une Meduse.

XXXI

Weightless Spirits, you who make your home
On earth or in the highest heavens roam,
Couriers of God, divine couriers who bear
His secrets in your circuits through the air:

Speak, couriers, speak (for thus no sorcerer
Can close you up within a ring of fire),
Skimming our fields, tell me, did you not see
That beauty who has waged such war on me?

If she by chance should see you here below,
Free through the air you never more shall go,
So subtle is her power to entrance.

Her beauty will transform you utterly,
Reduce you to a slave, as it has me,
Like a Medusa, with a single glance.[6]

---

6. Lines 1-4: In Renaissance Neoplatonism, in a tradition deriving ultimately from Hesiod's *Theogony* and *Works and Days*, the *daimonia* are spirits that intercede between gods and men. I have rendered Ronsard's "Démons" as "spirits" because "demons" in English is misleading and "daimons" awkward.

5-6: The sorcerer and his ring of fire pertains to the realm of Black Magic; thus we have an implicit *psychomachia*, or battle between good and wicked spirits, in the poem.

14: The Gorgon Medusa turned men to stone when they looked at her; she was eventually slain by the hero Perseus.

XXXII

Quand en naissant la Dame que j'adore,
De ses beautez vint embellir les cieux,
Le fils de Rhée appella tous les Dieux,
Pour faire d'elle encore une Pandore.

Lors Apollon de quatre dons l'honore,
Or' de ses rais luy façonnant les yeux,
Or' luy donnant son chant melodieux,
Or' son oracle et ses beaux vers encore.

Mars luy donna sa fiere cruauté,
Venus son ris, Dione sa beauté,
Pithon sa voix, Cerés son abondance,

L'Aube ses doits et ses crins deliés,
Amour son arc, Thetis donna ses piés,
Clion sa gloire, et Pallas sa prudence.

XXXII

When bringing forth the Lady I adore,
Whose many beauties ornament the skies,
The Son of Rhea called the deities
To make a new Pandora out of her.

The gifts Apollo deeds to her are four:
Now with his rays he fashions her clear eyes,
And now he gives his lovely melodies,
His oracle, the verse he holds in store.

Mars gave her his ferocious cruelty,
Venus gave smiles and laughter as her share,
Ceres abundance—its felicity,

The Dawn her fingers and her fine-spun hair,
Amor his bow, Dione beauty to spare,
Thetis her feet, Pallas sagacity.[7]

---

7. Ronsard, in company with almost all Renaissance poets, always uses the Latin name for a Greek god if it differs from the Greek name.

3: The Son of Rhea is Jupiter.

4: Pandora means "all gifted" in the Greek; the story of Pandora, the first woman, is told in Hesiod's *Works and Days*.

5: Apollo is associated, among other things, with poetry and prophecy.

9-11: Mars is the god of war; Venus (Aphrodite) in the *Theogony* is associated with "smiles and laughter"; and Ceres personifies the vegetative world and is associated with abundance. I have not translated Ronsard's phrase "Pithon sa voix," where he refers to Peitho, the goddess of persuasion (but see Sonnet II of *Les amours de Marie*).

13-14: Dione, whom Ronsard calls Clion, is associated with beauty in the *Theogony*. Hesiod's epithet for Thetis in the same work is "silver-footed." Pallas, an epithet of uncertain meaning for Athena, is known for her wisdom.

XXXVI

Pour la douleur qu'Amour veut que je sente,
Ainsi que moy Phebus tu lamentois,
Quand amoureux et banny tu chantois
Pres d'Ilion sur les rives de Xante.

Pinçant en vain ta lyre blandissante,
Fleuves et fleurs et bois tu enchantois,
Non la beauté qu'en l'ame tu sentois,
Qui te navroit d'une playe aigrissante.

Là de ton teint tu pallissois les fleurs,
Là les ruisseaux s'augmontoyent de tes pleurs,
Là tu vivois d'une esperance vaine.

Pour mesme nom Amour me fait douloir
Pres de Vandôme au rivage du Loir,
Comme un Phenis renaissant de ma peine.

XXXVI

In the same way, Phoebus, you used to bewail
The sadness that Love now decrees that I feel,
When lovesick and banished you sang on the shores
Of the Xanthus, fair river near Ilion's towers.

Plucking your blandishing lyre in vain,
Streams, flowers, and woods you enchanted again
And again, but the beauty that made your soul wounded
Was not moved at all by the music you sounded.

There, from your pallor the flowers were made pale;
There, from your tears would the rivulets swell;
There, your vain hopes made you live in despair.

Now Love makes me grieve for the very same name—
Near the town of Vendôme on the shores of the Loir,
Like a Phoenix reborn from my sorrow's own flame.[8]

---

8. The translation is in anapestic tetrameter. For a discussion of this poem, see the Introduction. Ronsard is making use—in a very general way, and only insofar as it allows for a comparison with the object of his own desire—of the story in which Apollo promises Cassandra, the daughter of King Priam and Queen Hecuba, the gift of prophecy if she will lie with him. She agrees, but, having received the gift, goes back on her word. To punish her, Apollo ensures that Cassandra's prophecies will never be believed. The story is told in Aeschylus's *Agamemnon*.

1: Phoebus, meaning "bright," is one of the epithets of Apollo.

4: The Xanthus, another name for the Scamander, is the river that runs through Troy in the *Iliad*.

5-11: Here Ronsard conflates Apollo with Orpheus, the archetypal poet.

13: Vendôme, the town in which Ronsard was born, is in central France; it lies on the River Loir (not to be confused with the much larger Loire).

14: When the Phoenix dies it is reborn out of its own ashes.

XL

Que de Beautez que de Graces écloses
Voy-je au jardin de ce sein verdelet
Enfler son rond de deux gazons de lait,
Où des Amours les fleches sont encloses!

Je me transforme en cent metamorfoses,
Quand je te voy petit mont jumelet,
Ains du printemps un rosier nouvelet,
Qui le matin caresse de ses roses.

S'Europe avoit l'estomach aussi beau,
Sage tu pris le masque d'un toreau,
Bon Jupiter pour traverser les ondes.

Le Ciel n'est dit parfait pour sa grandeur.
Luy et ce sein le sont pour leur rondeur:
Car le parfait consiste en choses rondes.

XL

What Beauties and what Graces can be seen
Blooming this garden's breast of youthful green;
And where twin plots of milky lawn are swelling
The Cupids with their little barbs are dwelling.

I undergo a hundred changes too
When, little double mound, I look at you,
As does a rosebush that a breeze discloses
When it caresses morning with its roses.

If Europa's breast was quite this beautiful,
You wisely took the semblance of a bull,
Good Jupiter, in traveling through the sea.

Not solely for its grandeur is the sky
Deemed perfect but, like this, for being round:
In roundness is perfection to be found.[9]

---

9. Line 4: The Cupids are known in Greeks mythology as the *Erotes* (followers of Eros).

14: The association between roundness and perfection is an ancient one.

XLIII

Ores la crainte et ores l'esperance
De tous costez se campent en mon cœur:
Ny l'un ny l'autre au combat n'est vainqueur,
Pareils en force et en perseverance.

Ores douteux, ores pleins d'asseurance,
Entre l'espoir le soupçon et la peur,
Pour estre en vain de moy-mesme trompeur,
Au cœur captif je promets delivrance.

Verray-je point avant mourir le temps,
Que je tondray la fleur de son printemps,
Sous qui ma vie à l'ombrage demeure?

Verray-je point qu'en ses bras enlassé,
Recreu d'amour, tout penthois et lassé,
D'un beau trespas entre ses bras je meurs?

XLIII

Now fear, now hope is dwelling in my heart,
Each in its turn encamped in every part:
Equal in perseverance and in power,
Neither can be the other's conqueror.

Now full of confidence, now racked with dread,
Suspecting hope, of fear itself afraid,
I promise my captive heart to set it free,
Fooling myself in my duplicity.

Shall I not see, before I die, the time
When I shall pluck the flower of her prime,
She who has made me languish in the shade?

Exhausted from love's ardors, still entwined
Within her arms, breathless, shall I not find
In such delights the blessings of the dead?[10]

---

10. Line 11 ("Sous qui ma vie à l'ombrage demeure?") is ambiguous in the French: it conveys the idea of "in the shade" (or "shadows") but also "as a shade." The point is that by making him languish in the shade—i.e. consigning him to the shadows—Cassandra has made him live as if he were a shade.

14: Ronsard's phrase "D'un beau trespas" ("From a beautiful death," or "passage out of the world") has the same metaphorical connection to orgasm that the Elizabethan "dying" has.

XLIV

Je voudrois estre Ixion et Tantale,
Dessus la roue et dans les eaux là bas,
Et nu à nu presser entre mes bras
Ceste beauté qui les anges égale.

S'ainsin estoit, toute peine fatale
Me seroit douce et ne me chaudroit pas
Non, d'un vautour fussé-je le repas,
Non, qui le roc remonte et redevale.

Voir ou toucher le rond de son tetin
Pourroit changer mon amoureux destin
Aux majestez des Princes de l'Asie:

Un demy-dieu me feroit son baiser,
Et sein sur sein mon feu desembraser,
Un de ces Dieux qui mangent l'Ambrosie.

XLIV

I'd gladly be Ixion on his wheel
Or Tantalus in the waters down below,
If I could hold her naked and could know
That beauty even the angels can't excel.

No torments sent by fate, if that were so—
Even the rock I had to push uphill
That always rolled back down—would lay me low,
Even the vulture making of me a meal.

To touch her rounded breast—or even see—
Would lift me from a lover's destiny
Unto the majesty of kings of Asia.

Her kiss would make a demi-god of me,
And skin to skin, my fire quenched, I'd be
One of those deities that eat ambrosia.[11]

---

11. Line 2: Zeus punished Tantalus by making him stand in a pool of water beneath a fruit tree: when he tried to eat, the fruit eluded his grasp, and when he tried to drink, the water receded.

5-8: Sisyphus was punished by being made perpetually to push a rock uphill, and Prometheus by having his liver eaten daily by an eagle after it had regenerated during the night.

14: Ambrosia is the food of the gods.

L

Cent fois le jour esbahi je repense,
Que c'est qu'Amour, quelle humeur l'entretient,
Quel est son arc, et quelle place il tient
Dedans nos cœurs, et quelle est son essence.

Je cognoy bien des astres l'influence,
Comme la mer toujours fuit et revient,
Comme en son tout le monde se contient:
Seule me fuit d'Amour la cognoissance.

Je suis certain qu'il est un puissant Dieu,
Et que, mobile, ores il prend son lieu
Dedans mon cœur, et ores dans mes veines:

Que de nature il ne fait jamais bien,
Qu'il porte un fruit dont le goust ne vault rien,
Et duquel l'arbre est tout chargé de peines.

L

Amazed, I think—a hundred times a day—
On Love, what mood sustains him, makes him stay,
What place he holds within these hearts of ours,
And what his essence is and what his powers.

That stars have influence, I know this well,
And that the sea will always ebb and swell;
I know that all things gather in the One;
But Love eludes me and remains unknown.

I'm certain that he is a puissant God,
That, changeable, he sometimes makes abode
Within my heart and sometimes in my veins;

That his effects are never of the best,
The fruit he bears being sour to the taste,
Its tree weighed down with sorrows and with pains.[12]

---

12. Line 7 in the French ("Comme en son tout le monde se contient"—literally: "As in its totality the world is contained") is both ambiguous and obscure. I have chosen to make what I think is Ronsard's implicit philosophical conception explicit.

LII

Avant qu'Amour du Chaos ocieux
Ouvrist le sein qui couvoit la lumiere
Avec la terre, avec l'onde premiere,
Sans art sans forme estoyent brouillez les Cieux.

Tel mon esprit à rien industrieux,
Dedans mon corps, lourde et grosse matiere,
Erroit sans forme et sans figure entiere,
Quand l'arc d'Amour le perça par tes yeux.

Amour rendit ma nature parfaite,
Pure par luy mon essence s'est faite,
Il me donna la vie et le pouvoir,

Il eschaufa tout mon sang de sa flame,
Et m'agitant de son vol feit mouvoir
Avecques luy mes pensers et mon ame.

LII

Before Love opened up the sluggish womb
Of Chaos, which had not yet given birth
To light or to the waters and the earth,
The Heavens were turbulent and without form.

Likewise my spirit, lacking enterprise,
Within my body's gross and heavy matter,
Aimlessly wandered without form or feature
Till Love's keen arrows pierced it through your eyes.

My nature was transformed and made complete
By Love; through him my being was made pure;
He gave me life and with it gave me power.

He heated up my blood with his strong flame,
And setting me in motion in his flight
He made my thoughts and feelings move with him.[13]

---

13. Lines 1-4: Chaos, meaning "chasm" and gendered female in Hesiod's *Theogony*, is the first of things and gives birth to all others.

9: The French adjective "parfait" retains its Latinate sense of "complete" for Ronsard.

LVII

Divin Bellay, dont les nombreuses lois
Par un ardeur du peuple separée,
Ont revestu l'enfant de Cytherée
D'arcs, de flambeaux, de traits, et de carquois:

Si le doux feu dont jeune tu ardois,
Enflambe encor ta poitrine sacrée,
Si ton oreille encore se recrée,
D'ouir les plaints des amoureuses vois:

Oy ton Ronsard qui sanglote et lamente,
Pale de peur, pendu sur la tourmente,
Croizant en vain ses mains devers les Cieux,

En fraile nef, sans mast, voile ne rame,
Et loin du havre où pour astre Madame
Me conduisoit du Fare de ses yeux.

LVII

Divine Bellay, whose laws of prosody,
Through a people's ardent spirit lifted high,
Have clothed the child of Cythera anew
With bows, with torches, arrows, quivers too:

If the sweet fire that kindled you with flame,
Within your sacred breast still burns the same,
And if, as in your youth, your ear rejoices
At hearing the laments of lovers' voices,

Then hear your Ronsard sobbing his complaint
In torments of suspense, who, pale and faint,
Crosses his hands in vain before the Skies,

In a frail bark with neither sail nor oar,
And far from harbor, where instead of star
He's led by the beacon of his Lady's eyes.[14]

---

14. Lines 1-2: Joachim Du Bellay (1522-60) was co-leader of the Pléiade with Ronsard. An exceptional poet who was translated in the sixteenth century by Edmund Spenser, Du Bellay was the theorist of the group, and in this sonnet's opening lines Ronsard alludes to his manifesto (to which Ronsard himself may have contributed), *Déffense et illustration de la langue française* (1549). (Richard Helgerson in the preface to his translation of Du Bellay's *The Regrets* [Philadelphia: University of Pennsylvania Press, 2006] has cogently argued that the title of Du Bellay's manifesto should be translated as "Defense and Enrichment of the French Language" [xi].) The French phrase in line 1, "nombreuses lois," which I translate as "laws of prosody," means both "numerous laws" and "laws of number" —i.e. versification: the point is that Du Bellay has expounded in detail the rules and principles pertaining to poetry. Ronsard implies, moreover, that Du Bellay's renovation of French poetry via the classics will lead to a political renovation of France as a nation; thus in line 2, the "people's ardent spirit lifted high" is both a response to the new poetry of the Pléiade and what inspires that poetry.

3-4: Cythera is an island sacred to Venus; thus, by a frequently used metonymy, the "child of Cythera" is Amor (Eros), or, as Ronsard usually refers to him, Amour—Love. In Ronsard's complex metaphor, du Bellay has "clothed the child of Cythera anew" by giving love the potential for new expression in the language of the vernacular.

LVIII

Quand le Soleil à chef renversé plonge
Son char doré dans le sein du vieillard,
Et que la nuit un bandeau sommeillard
Mouillé d'oubly dessus nos yeux alonge:

Amour adonc qui sape mine et ronge
De ma raison le chancellant rempart,
Comme un guerrier en diligence part,
Armant son camp des ombres et du songe.

Lors ma raison et lors ce Dieu cruel,
Seuls per à per d'un choc continuel
Vont redoublant mille escarmouches fortes:

Si bien qu'Amour n'en seroit le veinqueur
Sans mes pensers qui luy ouvrent les portes,
Tant mes soudars sont traistres à mon cueur.

LVIII

When, with his head thrown back, the Sun goes down,
Plunging his golden chariot in the deep,
And Night has stretched a blindfold soaked in sleep
Over our eyes, bringing oblivion,

Love, which erodes and undermines the beams
Of my frail reason so its ramparts stagger,
Sets off in haste, and with a warrior's swagger,
To arm his camp with shadows and with dreams.

My reason and that cruel God are then
Locked into single combat in a war
Of skirmishes that still prolong my pain.

Nor yet would Love emerge as conqueror,
Did not my thoughts open up Reason's fort:
So treacherous are my soldiers to my heart.[15]

---

15. Line 2: What I have rendered as "the deep" is in the French "le sein du vieillard": literally, "the bosom of the old man"—which is to say, the Old Man of the Sea, or Ocean (the god Okeanos).

LIX

Comme un Chevreuil, quand le printemps détruit
Du froid hyver la poignante gelée,
Pour mieux brouter la fueille emmielée,
Hors de son bois avec l'Aube s'enfuit:

Et seul, et seur, loin de chiens et de bruit,
Or' sur un mont, or' dans une valée,
Or' pres d'une onde à l'escart recelée,
Libre, folastre où son pié le conduit:

De rets ne d'arc sa liberté n'a crainte
Sinon alors que sa vie est attainte
D'un trait meurtrier empourpré de son sang.

Ainsi j'alloy sans espoir de dommage,
Le jour qu'un œil sur l'Avril de mon âge
Tira d'un coup mille traits en mon flanc.

LIX

Just as the roebuck, when the spring destroys
The piercing ice and winter's chill is gone,
Better to browse on honeyed foliage, flies
Out of its native woods at break of dawn:

Alone, in safety, far from horns and hounds,
Now in a valley, now atop a hill,
Now near remote, secluded pools it bounds,
Frolicking free and wandering where it will:

Of net or bow, its freedom has no dread—
Until the moment when it's halted by
A murderous arrow which its blood stains red.

Thus, without fear of harm I went my way,
Till in the April of my age, one day,
I was struck down by bolts shot from her eye.[16]

---

16. Line 14: The arrows (or bolts) shot from the beloved's eye is a frequently used Petrarchan conceit.

LXVIII

L'œil qui rendroit le plus barbare appris,
Qui tout orgueil en humblesse détrempe,
Et qui subtil affine de sa trempe
Le plus terrestre et lourd de nos espris,

M'a tellement de ses beautez épris,
Qu'autre beauté dessus mon cœur ne rampe,
Et m'est avis, sans voir un jour la lampe
De ces beaux yeux, que la mort me tient pris.

Cela que l'air est de propre aux oiseaux,
Les bois aux cerfs, et aux poissons les eaux,
Son bel œil m'est. Ô lumiere enrichie

D'un feu divin qui m'ard si vivement,
Pour me donner l'estre et le mouvement,
Este-vous pas ma seule Entelechie?

LXVIII

The eye that taught the barbarous soul to see,
Tempering arrogance through humility,
And subtly stamped its character upon
Carnal proclivities that weigh us down,

Has seized me with its lovely qualities
(No other beauty can compare with these),
And warns me that were I to lose one day
The lamp of those fair eyes, I'd be death's prey.

Just as the air remains the proper sphere
For birds, water for fish, and woods for deer,
Her lovely eye is mine. O light containing

Fire divine that burns so ardently,
Giving me movement and my very being,
Are you not then my sole Entelechy?[17]

---

17. Line 14: Entelechy (*entelecheia*) in Aristotle's metaphysics is a form-giving cause: that which realizes what is otherwise merely potential.

LXXXI

Pardonne moy, Platon, si je ne cuide
Que sous le rond de la voute des Dieux,
Sois hors du monde, ou au profond des lieux
Que Styx entourne, il n'y ait quelque vuide.

Si l'air est plein en sa voute liquide,
Qui reçoit donc tant de pleurs de mes yeux,
Tant de soupirs que je sanglote aux cieux,
Lors qu'à mon dueil Amour lasche la bride?

Il est du vague, ou si point il n'en est,
D'un air pressé le comblement ne naist:
Plus-tost le ciel, qui piteux se dispose

À recevoir l'effet de mes douleurs,
De toutes parts se comble de mes pleurs,
Et de mes vers qu'en mourant je compose.

LXXXI

Pardon me, Plato, if I can't assume
That under the round vault of the Gods, outside
The world, maybe, or in the deepest gloom
That Styx encompasses, there's not some void.

If a plenum exists in that vault, does the flow
Come from the tears that pour from my eyes
As well as the sighs I sob to the skies
When Love slacks the reins that bridle my woe?

It's indeterminate, remains unclear
If the filling-up proceeds from pressed-in air,
Or if the sky takes pity and is disposed

To gather in my sorrows and my cares,
Till all its parts are filled up with my tears
And verses—those in dying I've composed.[18]

---

18. The translation varies between iambic and anapestic rhythms and between a pentameter and tetrameter measure.

Lines 1-5: Probably purely for the sake of the metaphorical conception he is developing, Ronsard questions Plato's support in the *Timaeus* for what came to be known as the *plenum*—that is, the idea that space is filled with matter of some kind, and hence that "Nature abhors a vacuum." The Stoics, following the lead of Proclus, believed that space is a substance that fills everything.

4: The Styx is one of the five rivers of Hades.

XCIV

Soit que son or se crespe lentement,
Ou soit qu'il vague en deux glissantes ondes,
Qui çà qui là par le sein vagabondes,
Et sur le col nagent follastrement:

Ou soit qu'un noud illustré richement
De maints rubis et maintes perles rondes,
Serre les flots de ses deux tresses blondes,
Mon cueur se plaist en son contentement.

Quel plaisir est-ce, ainçois quelle merveille,
Quand ses cheveux troussez dessus l'oreille,
D'une Venus imitent la façon?

Quand d'un bonnet sa teste elle Adonise,
Et qu'on ne sçait s'elle est fille ou garçon,
Tant sa beauté en tous deux se desguise?

XCIV

Whether her golden hair in gentle curls
Floats, or in wavy double-plaits unfurls,
Playfully roaming here and there, now pressed
Against her neck or billowing on her breast:

Or whether her two blonde tresses have been bound
With rubies and with pearls both rich and round
Into a knot that ornaments its treasure,
My heart rejoices and expands with pleasure.

What joy she gives, how marvelous appears,
When with her hair bunched up above her ears,
She comes upon us in the form of Venus.

But whether she's girl or boy no one can tell—
Her beauty takes on either guise so well—
When in a cap she imitates Adonis.[19]

---

19. Line 14: Adonis, an extraordinarily handsome youth who was the mortal lover of Venus, died after being gored by a wild boar. In the story told by Ovid in Book 10 of the *Metamorphoses*, he was conceived as a result of the incestuous union of Myrrha and her father.

CIV

Devant les yeux nuict et jour me revient
Le saint portrait de l'angelique face:
Soit que j'escrive, ou soit que j'entrelasse
Mes vers au Luth, tousjours il m'en souvient.

Voyez pour Dieu, comme un bel œil me tient
En sa prison, et point ne me delasse:
Comme mon cœur il empestre en sa nasse,
Qui de pensée, à mon dam l'entretient.

Ô le grand mal, quand nostre ame est saisie
Des monstres naiz dedans la fantaisie!
Le jugement est toujours en prison.

Amour trompeur, pourquoy me fais-tu croire
Que la blancheur est une chose noire,
Et que les sens sont plus que la raison!

CIV

Both night and day, before those eyes I see
The saintly portrait of the angelic face:
And if I write, and if I interlace
Lines to the lute, it's in my memory.

For God's sake, see how that same lovely eye
Imprisons me and offers me no peace:
My heart's entangled and the web I trace
Sustained by thought—to my great injury.

How painful is the spirit's subjugation
To monsters born in the imagination!
Our judgment then is always held in prison.

Deceiving Love, why do you make me think
That whiteness is a thing as black as ink,
And that the senses hold more truth than reason!

CXIX

D'Amour ministre, et de perseverance,
Qui jusqu'au fond l'ame peux esmouvoir,
Et qui les yeux d'un aveugle sçavoir,
Et qui les cœurs voiles d'une ignorance:

Va t'en ailleurs chercher ta demeurance,
Va t'en ailleurs quelqu'autre decevoir:
Je ne veux plus chez moy te recevoir,
Malencontreuse et maudite esperance.

Quand Jupiter, ce Tyran criminel,
Teignit ses mains dans le sang paternel,
Dérobant l'or de la terre où nous sommes,

Il te laissa, comme un monstre nouveau,
Seule par force au profond du vaisseau
Que Pandore eut pour decevoir les hommes.

CXIX

Servant of Love and perseverance, who
Can move unto its very depths the soul,
And, blind to knowledge, who can spread a veil
Of ignorance upon men's hearts also:

Go elsewhere for your dwelling-place; yes, go
Some other place to trick some other man:
No longer do I want to take you in,
Unlucky hope—accursed in being so.

When Jupiter, felonious tyrant, dipped
His hands in the paternal blood and stripped
The gold from this same earth, our habitation,

He left you, as a monstrous new creation,
Alone within the vessel's depths—the one
Given Pandora to deceive poor men.[20]

---

20. Lines 9-11: In Book 1 of Ovid's *Metamorphoses*, when Saturn (Kronos) is supplanted by Jupiter (Zeus), the Golden Age comes to an end.

12-14: In the story told by Hesiod in the *Works and Days*, hope is the only thing that remains in the jar after Pandora has opened it and released all of the evils of the world.

CXX

Franc de raison, esclave de fureur,
Je vay chassant une Fere sauvage,
Or' sur un mont, or' le long d'un rivage,
Or' dans le bois de jeunesse et d'erreur.

J'ai pour ma lesse un long trait de malheur,
J'ay pour limier un violent courage:
J'ay pour mes chiens, l'ardeur, et le jeune âge,
Et pour piqueurs, l'espoir et la douleur.

Mais eux voyans, que plus elle est chassee,
Plus elle fuit d'une course eslancee,
Quittent leur proye: et retournent vers moy

De ma chair propre osant bien leur repaistre.
C'est grand pitié (à mon dam je le voy)
Quand les valets commandent à leur maistre.

CXX

Being unconstrained by reason, passion's thrall,
I go to chase a savage animal,
Now on a mountain, now along a river,
Now in the wood of youth and childish error.

The leash I hold is misery's long rope,
Determination is my bloodhound fierce,
My dogs are ardency and youthful years,
My whippers-on are suffering and hope.

But seeing that the more that she is chased,
The more she flies away in headlong haste,
They quit their prey, and, coming back to me,

They even dare to make *me* their repast.
Oh what a pity (I see it to my cost)
When those that serve have gained the mastery![21]

---

21. This sonnet echoes the medieval-allegorical *hunt of love* tradition, which Ronsard may be deriving from Petrarch's canzone XXIII, "Nel dolce tempo de la prima etade" (see Grahame Castor, "Petrarchism and the Quest for Beauty in the *Amours* of Cassandre and the *Sonets pour Helene*," in *Ronsard the Poet*, ed. Terence Cave [London: Methuen & Co., 1973], 83-84). The sonnet alludes to the myth of Actaeon, who, having come upon Diana (Artemis) bathing with her nymphs, is punished by being turned to a stag and pursued and eaten by his dogs. Ovid tells the story in Book 3 of the *Metamorphoses*.

CXXIX

Di l'un des deux, sans tant me déguiser
Le peu d'amour que ton semblant me porte,
Je ne sçauroy, veu ma peine si forte,
Tant lamenter, ne tant Petrarquiser.

Si tu le veux, que sert de refuser
Ce doux present dont l'espoir me conforte?
Sinon, pourquoy d'une esperance morte
Me nourris-tu pour tousjours m'abuser?

L'un de tes yeux dans les enfers me rue,
L'autre plus doux à l'envy s'esvertue
De me remettre en paradis encor:

Ainsi tes yeux, pour causer mon renaistre,
Et puis ma mort, sans cesse me font estre
Or' un Pollux, et ores un Castor.

CXXIX

Say yes or no without so much disguising:
The lack of love I see upon your face
Gives me more grief than what I can express
In lamentation or in Petrarchizing.

Why, if it's what you want, refuse this sweet
Present, which even in thought allays my pain?
If not, why nourish hopes completely vain,
Hopes that you only starve in your deceit?

One eye would cast me into hell; her sister,
Gentler by far, is striving to resist her
And raising me once more to paradise.

They make me die and be reborn, your eyes,
Transforming me by turns and faster and faster
Into a Pollux now and now a Castor.[22]

---

22. Line 4: The Pléiade edition glosses "Petrarquiser" as "playing the entranced lover" ("faire de l'amoureux transi" [1.1256]). In any case, much as he is embedded in the Petrarchan tradition, Ronsard is here clearly breaking with what he sees as its artificiality and affectedness.

13: "Faster and faster" is my interpolation.

14: Castor and Pollux are the twin sons of Leda. In Homer's *Iliad* they are both mortal and both the sons of Leda's husband Tyndareus; but in Pindar, while Castor is mortal, Pollux is the immortal son of Zeus, the result of his rape of Leda. In one version of the myth, when Castor was dying, Zeus allowed Pollux to share his immortality with his brother; as a result, the two became the brightest stars in the constellation Gemini.

CXXXV

Douce beauté, meurdriere de ma vie,
En lieu d'un cœur tu portes un rocher:
Tu me fais vif languir et desecher,
Passionné d'une amoureuse envie.

Le jeune sang qui d'aimer te convie,
N'a peu de toy la froideur arracher,
Farouche fiere, et qui n'as rien plus cher
Que languir froide, et n'estre point servie.

Appren à vivre, ô fiere en cruauté:
Ne garde point à Pluton ta beauté,
Quelque peu d'aise en aimant il faut prendre.

Il faut tromper doucement le trespas:
Car aussi bien sous la terre là bas
Sans rien sentir le corps n'est plus que cendre.

CXXXV

Sweet beauty, murderess who murders me,
You have a stone, there where your heart should be;
You make me pine away—alive, I languish,
Enflamed by love and by love's bitter anguish.

The blood of youth that beckons you to love
Has failed to uproot your coldness or to move
You, who like nothing better, fierce and proud,
Than coldly languishing in solitude.

Learn how to live, most fierce and cruel of ladies:
Why should you keep your beauty only for Hades?
In love we can take some solace, as one must.

Gently we must cheat death before we go
Under the earth; for, surely, down below
The body has no feeling, is merely dust.[23]

---

23. Line 11: For Pluto (Ronsard's Pluton), the Roman name of the god of the underworld, I have substituted the Greek Hades.

CXLV

J'avois l'esprit tout morne et tout pesant,
Quand je receu du lieu qui me tourmente,
L'orenge d'or comme moy jaunissante
Du mesme mal qui nous est si plaisant.

Les Pommes sont de l'Amour le present:
Tu le sçais bien, ô guerriere Atalante,
Et Cydippé qui encor se lamente
De l'escrit d'or qui luy fut si cuisant.

Les Pommes sont de l'Amour le vray signe.
Heureux celuy qui de la pomme est digne!
Tousjours Venus a des pommes au sein.

Depuis Adam desireux nous en sommes:
Tousjours la Grace en a dedans la main,
Et bref l'Amour n'est qu'un beau jeu de pommes.

CXLV

My spirits were sunk in gloom and much I grieved
When from my place of torment I received
The golden fruit, grown yellow, as was I,
From the same sickness that gives so much joy.

The Apples are the gift that Love accords:
O warlike Atalanta, this you know;
And you, Cydippe, still have cause to rue
How piercing were the letter's golden words.

The Apples are Love's sign, and only he
That's worthy of the apple can be blessed!
Venus has always held them to her breast.

Since Adam, our desire for it's the same.
Each Grace has one in hand habitually,
And Love, in brief, is just an apple game.[24]

---

24. Line 3: Ronsard's phrase is literally, "the golden orange"; my sense, however, is that it is possible to conflate oranges and apples in sixteenth-century French and that this is what Ronsard in fact is doing. The "golden apple of discord" was thrown by Eris, the goddess of discord (or violence), to the gods and goddesses assembled at a feast for the wedding of Peleus and Thetis. It was awarded by Paris to Aphrodite and thus sparked the Trojan War. Hence the reference to Venus in line 11 below.

6: The virgin huntress Atalanta agreed to marry only someone who could defeat her in a footrace. Hippomenes tricked her by rolling apples in front of her each time she pulled ahead of him. By picking them up, she inadvertently allowed him to win the race. The story is told by Ovid in Book X of the *Metamorphoses*.

7: In a story told by Ovid in his *Heroïdes,* Acontius was enamored of Cydippe (pronounced Sigh-DIP-pee), an Athenian maiden. He wrote on an apple the words "I swear by Artemis that I will marry Acontius" and threw it at her feet. She picked it up and read the words out loud. Having thus taken a solemn vow, she was eventually obligated by the goddess to go through with the marriage.

13: The Graces (*Gratiae* in Latin, *Charites* in Greek) are goddesses associated with beauty, nature, love, and fertility. There is a painting by Raphael of the Three Graces, each of whom is holding an apple. Whether Ronsard had seen it or knew of its existence is an interesting question, but it is housed in France, at the Musée Condé of Chantilly. It is thought to have been executed between 1503 and 1505 and is the first painting in which Raphael depicted the nude female form in front and back views.

CLII

Lune à l'œil brun, Deesse aux noirs chevaux,
Qui çà, qui là qui haut qui bas te tournent,
Et de retours qui jamais ne sejournent,
Trainent ton char eternel en travaux:

À tes desirs les miens ne sont egaux,
Car les amours qui ton ame epoinçonnent,
Et les ardeurs qui la mienne eguillonnent,
Divers souhaits desirent à leurs maux.

Toy mignottant ton dormeur de Latmie,
Voudrois tousjours qu'une course endormie
Retint le train de ton char qui s'enfuit:

Mais moy qu'Amour toute la nuict devore,
Depuis le soir je souhaite l'Aurore,
Pour voir le jour, que me celoit ta nuit.

CLII

Brown-eyed Moon, goddess whose coal-black horses
Turn you hither and thither and high and low,
And never remaining where they return to or go,
Drag your chariot through its eternal courses:

The desire that is mine is not the same as yours is,
Because the loves that pierce your soul right through
And the passions enflaming mine and bringing it woe
Are different, have different wishes and different sources.

Caressing your sleeper on Latmos, you always keep
Hoping your chariot's progress, lulled by sleep,
Will be held back from speeding upon its flight:

But I, whom Love devours, am always yearning,
From evening on, to see Aurora dawning,
The daylight hidden from me by your night.[25]

---

25. Lines 1-11: According to a story told by Apollonius of Rhodes in the *Argonautica*, Selene, the Titan goddess of the moon, loved the shepherd Endymion. Seeing him asleep in a cave on Mount Latmos, she begged Zeus to have him remain this way, and each night visited the sleeping youth.

CLX

Or' que Jupin espoint de sa semence
Veux enfanter ses enfans bien-aimez,
Et que du chaud de ses reins allumez
L'humide sein de Junon ensemence:

Or' que la mer, or' que la vehemence
Des vents fait place aux grans vaisseaux armez,
Et que l'oiseau parmi les bois ramez,
Du Thracien les tançons recommence:

Or' que les prez et ore que les fleurs
De mille et mille et de mille couleurs
Peignent le sein de la terre si gaye,

Seul et pensif aux rochers plus segrets
D'un cœur muet je conte mes regrets,
Et par les bois je vay celant ma playe.

CLX

Now when great Jove in his virility
Wants to engender his dear progeny,
And from his burning loins spurts jets of spume,
Inseminating Juno's hot, wet womb:

Now when the sea, now when the winds so wild
And vehement, to great armadas yield,
Now when the bird amidst the forest's boughs
Against the Thracian her complaint renews:

Now when the meadows, when so many flowers,
With thousands upon thousands upon thousands of colors,
Are painting the bosom of the earth so gay,

Among secluded rocks, sad and apart,
I count my sorrows with a muffled heart:
Hiding my wounds, through woods I make my way.[26]

---

26. Line 1: Jove, among the Romans, is an alternate name for Jupiter (Zeus), the sky-god and father of the gods. Ronsard in line 1 refers to Jupiter as "Jupin," yet another name for the sky-god in sixteenth-century French.

4: Juno (Hera) is Jupiter's wife and consort.

7-8: The bird is the nightingale. Ronsard alludes to the story of Philomela, who, having been raped by Tereus, the king of Thrace and the husband of her sister Procne, is transformed to a nightingale while Procne becomes a swallow. The story is told in Book 6 of Ovid's *Metamorphoses*.

CLXV

Sainte Gastine, ô douce secretaire
De mes ennuis, qui respons en ton bois,
Ores en haute ore en basse voix,
Aux longs souspirs que mon cœur ne peut taire:

Loir, qui refreins la course volontaire
Des flots roulans par nostre Vandomois,
Quand accuser ceste beauté tu m'ois,
De qui tousjours je m'affame et m'altere:

Si dextrement l'augure j'ay receu,
Et si mon œil ne fut hier deceu
Des doux regards de ma douce Thalie,

Maugré la mort Poëte me ferez
Et par la France appellez vous serez
L'un mon Laurier, l'autre ma Castalie.

CLXV

Holy Gastine, what memories you impart
Of all my griefs—they echo through your wood,
Now in high tones, now in a voice subdued,
To sighs that can't be silenced by my heart:

Loir, who restrain the current, for your part,
Rolling through our Vendômian neighborhood,
When you have heard my accusations flood
Against one who has starved me from the start:

If ably I received the augury,
And wasn't blinded yesterday or gulled
In my sweet visions of my Thalia,

Then, spite of death, you'll make a Poet of me,
And by all France you henceforth shall be called
My Laurel and my sweet Castalia.[27]

---

27. Lines 1-6: The Gastine Forest is in the neighborhood of Vendôme, the town in central France where Ronsard was born. The River Loir runs through the area.

11: Thalia is the Muse of Comedy—though here Ronsard seems less interested in her association with comedy than in the fact that she is a muse and in the rhyme of "Thalie" with "Castalie."

14: That is, the Gastine will be his laurel and the Loir his Castalian spring. Apollo tried to seduce Daphne, who was transformed by her father, the River Peneus, into a laurel tree. Apollo then crowned himself with laurel, which, in consequence, becomes associated with poetry. The story is told in Book 1 of Ovid's *Metamorphoses*. The nymph Castalia was transformed by Apollo into a spring at Delphi, at the base of Mount Parnassus. The Castalian Spring is sacred to the Muses.

CLXXII

Je veux brusler, pour m'en-voler aux cieux,
Tout l'imparfait de mon escorce humaine,
M'éternisant comme le fils d'Alcméne,
Qui tout en feu s'assit entre les Dieux.

Ja mon esprit desireux de son mieux,
Dedans ma chair, rebelle, se promeine,
Et ja le bois de sa victime ameine
Pour s'immoler aux rayons de tes yeux.

Ô saint brazier, ô flame entretenue
D'un feu divin, avienne que ton chaud
Brusle si bien ma despouille connue,

Que libre et nu je vole d'un plein saut
Outre le ciel, pour adorer là haut
L'autre beauté dont la tienne est venue.

CLXXII

To rise up to the heavens I want a flame
That burns corruption from my human frame
And makes me immortal like great Hercules,
Who blazed among the Olympian deities.

Already my spirit, desiring its own good,
Rebellious to my body, bears the wood
On which the victim of the sacrifice
Will be consumed in the rays from your eyes.

O flame that is fed by a heavenly fire,
May it come to pass that your heat, sacred pyre,
Burns the familiar old skin I have worn,

Till, naked and free, with one bound I can fly
Out beyond the ether, to adore up on high
That other beauty from which yours has been born.[28]

---

28. Lines 3-4: After having been mistakenly poisoned by his wife Deianira, when he put on the shirt that the Centaur Nessus had dipped in the blood of the Hydra, the dying Hercules (Herakles) prepared his own funeral pyre. His immortal half remained unburned by the flames, and in an apotheosis he was taken up by Zeus to the Olympian gods. Ronsard uses the story as a metaphor to create a Platonic myth of transcendence.

3: Hercules was the son of Jupiter and a mortal woman, Alcmene ("le fils d'Alcméne" in the French).

14: "That other beauty" is Beauty as a Platonic form (but not capitalized in the French in this instance).

CLXXIII

Mon fol penser pour s'en-voler plus haut
Apres le bien que hautain je desire,
S'est emplumé d'ailes jointes de cire,
Propres à fondre au rais du premier chaud.

Luy fait oiseau, dispost de saut en saut
Poursuit en vain l'objet de son martire,
Et toy qui peux et luy dois contredire,
Tu le vois bien, Raison, et ne t'en chaut.

Sous la clarté d'une estoile si belle
Cesse, Penser, de hazarder ton aile,
Qu'on ne te voye en bruslant desplumer:

Pour amortir une ardeur si cuisante,
L'eau de mes yeux ne seroit suffisante,
Ny l'eau du ciel, ny les flots de la mer.

CLXXIII

My foolish thought, to make itself soar higher,
After the highest good which I desire,
Has feathered itself with wings attached with wax,
Wings that will surely melt when the hot sun bakes.

Changed to a bird, it nimbly flits—in vain,
Seeking the very thing that gives it pain;
And you who can and ought to intercede,
You see it, Reason, yet you pay no heed.

Don't risk your wing, O Thought, by taking flight
Beneath the radiance of a star so bright,
Lest that your feathers be consumed by fire.

To quench such burning ardor would require
More than the water streaming from my eyes,
More than the rain, more than the briny seas.[29]

---

29. Lines 3-4: Ronsard is here alluding to the story of Icarus, who, having received from his father Daedalus wings attached to his arms with wax, flew too close to the sun, and, when the wax melted, fell into the sea.

CLXXIV

Or' que le ciel, or' que la terre est pleine
De glas, de gresle esparse en tous endrois,
Et que l'horreur des plus froidureux mois
Fait herisser les cheveux de la plaine:

Or' que le vent qui mutin se promeine,
Rompt les rochers, et desplante les bois,
Et que la mer redoublant ses abois,
Sa rage enflee aux rivages ameine:

Amour me brusle, et l'hyver froidureux,
Qui gele tout, de mon feu chaleureux
Ne gele point l'ardeur qui tousjours dure.

Voyez, Amans, comme je suis traité,
Je meurs de froid au plus chaud de l'esté,
Et de chaleur au cœur de la froidure.

CLXXIV

Now when the sky, now when the earth is filled
With ice, and hail is splattering every street,
Now when the hair-like grasses of the field
Are stiffening and bristling with sleet;

Now when unruly winds are on the prowl,
Uprooting ancient tree-trunks by the score,
And when the sea, repeating howl on howl,
Inflicts its swollen rage upon the shore:

Love scorches me; the everlasting ardor
That always burns within me burns the harder
When all things else are freezing everywhere.

Lovers, take note: you see how well I fare:
I die of cold the hotter summer blazes,
Of heat in the heart of winter when it freezes.

CLXXX

Amour et Mars sont presque d'une sorte:
L'un en plein jour, l'autre combat de nuit,
L'un aux rivaux, l'autre aux gendarmes nuit,
L'un rompt un huis, l'autre rompt une porte.

L'un finement trompe une ville forte,
L'autre coiment une maison seduit:
L'un le butin, l'autre le gain poursuit,
L'un deshonneur, l'autre dommage apporte.

L'un couche à terre, et l'autre gist souvent
Devant un huis à la froideur du vent:
L'un boit mainte eau, l'autre boit mainte larme.

Mars va tout seul, les Amours vont tous seuls:
Qui voudra donc ne languir paresseux,
Soit l'un ou l'autre, amoureux, ou gendarme.

CLXXX

Amor and Mars are almost of the same sort:
The one in plain day, the other does combat at night;
One battles with rivals, and one with dark warriors of might;
One breaks down a door, the other shatters a fort:

One subtly tricks a strong city through treason or art,
The other seduces a household, destroying it quite;
One's quest is for gain, the other seeks booty more slight;
The one brings dishonor, the other does harm, for its part.

One sleeps on the ground, the other you'll frequently find
In front of a door—in the teeth of a fearsome wind;
The one drinks much water, the other drinks many a tear.

Mars is a loner; the Cupids all go it alone:
If you don't want to languish in sloth, you must strive to be known
As one or the other, a lover or man of war.[30]

---

30. The translation varies between iambic and anapestic pentameter.
Line 1: Amor and Mars: the gods of love and war.

CXCII

Il faisoit chaud, et le somne coulant
Se distilloit dans mon ame songearde,
Quand l'incertain d'une idole gaillarde
Fut doucement mon dormir affolant.

Panchant sous moy son bel ivoyre blanc,
Et m'y tirant sa langue fretillarde,
Me baizottoit d'une lévre mignarde,
Bouche sur bouche, et le flanc sur le flanc.

Que de coral, que de liz, que de roses,
Ce me sembloit à pleines mains descloses
Tastay-je lors entre deux maniments?

Mon Dieu, mon Dieu, de quelle douce haleine,
De quelle odeur estoit sa bouche pleine,
De quels rubis, et de quels diamans?

CXCII

The day was hot, and flowing slumber seeped
Into my dreaming soul, and as I slept
The hazy outline of a sprite took shape
Gently in my infatuated sleep.

Lovely her ivory whiteness as she clung
Tightly to me and offered me a tongue
Darting from dainty little lips in play,
As mouth upon mouth, body on body we lay.

Coral and roses, lilies—all these seemed
To fall into my grasp the while I dreamed:
How much I felt and touched with open hands.

My God, my God, how sweetly was revealed
The honeyed scent with which her mouth was filled.
What rubies spilled out and what diamonds.[31]

---

31. Line 3: The phrase that I have translated as "a sprite" in the French is "une idole gaillarde" (literally: "a lusty idol").

CXCIII

Ces flots jumeaux de laict bien espoissi
Vont et revont par leur blanche valée,
Comme à son bord la marine salée,
Qui lente va, lente revient aussi.

Une distance entre eux se fait, ainsi
Qu'entre deux monts une sente égalée,
Blanche par tout de neige devalée,
Quand en hyver le vent s'est adouci.

Là deux rubis haut eslevez rougissent,
Dont les rayons cet ivoyre finissent
De toutes parts uniment arrondis:

Là tout honneur, là toute grace abonde:
Et la beauté, si quelqu'une est au monde,
Vole au sejour de ce beau paradis.

CXCIII

These two twin streams of clotted milk that flow
Over a valley white itself as snow—
They are like tides approaching near the shore,
Which slowly ebb and slowly flow back once more.

A space between them forms, as if between
Hills, where a leveled pathway can be seen,
White from the drifts of snow with which it's filled—
In winter, when the wind drops and is stilled.

Two gleaming rubies there are raised on high:
They lend their radiance to the ivory
That smoothly curves around them on all sides.

All honor there, and there all grace abides;
And beauty, if the world has any, flies
To the abode of this fair paradise.[32]

---

32. For a discussion of this sonnet, see the Introduction.

CCXXVII

Le Jeu, la Grace, et les Freres jumeaux
Suivent ma Dame, et quelque part qu'elle erre,
Dessous ses pieds fait esmailler la terre,
Et des hyvers fait des printemps nouveaux.

En sa faveur jargonnent les oiseaux,
Ses vents Eole en sa caverne enserre,
Le doux Zephyre un doux soupir desserre,
Et tous muets s'accoisent les ruisseaux.

Les Elemens se remirent en elle,
Nature rit de voir chose si belle:
Je tremble tout, que quelqu'un de ces Dieux

Ne passionne apres son beau visage,
Et qu'en pillant le tresor de nostre âge,
Ne la ravisse et ne l'emporte aux cieux.

CCXXVII

With Mirth and Grace the amorous Brothers twain
Follow my Lady: everywhere she goes,
Beneath her feet, the earth's adorned, and throws
Off winter to bring springtime back again.

In praise of her the birds sing their refrain,
And Aeolus's winds in caves repose;
Sweet Zephyrus with sweet breath a soft sigh blows;
Rivers are mute—from roaring they refrain.

The Elements behold themselves in her,
And Nature smiles to see a thing so fair:
I tremble lest one of those Deities,

Impassioned by her visage, in wild rage,
And plundering the treasure of our age,
Should ravish her and bear her to the skies.[33]

---

33. Line 1: The twin brothers ("Freres jumeaux") are the *Erotes* (or Loves), followers of Venus and Cupid.

6: Aeolus in Book 10 of Homer's *Odyssey* is the keeper of the winds. He gives Odysseus a favorable wind and a bag containing unfavorable winds, but Odysseus's men open the bag and Odysseus is blown back to Aeolus, who then refuses to provide another favorable wind.

7: Zephyrus is the west wind.

CCXXIX

J'alloy roulant ces larmes de mes yeux,
Or' plein de doute ore plein d'esperance,
Lors que Henry loing des bornes de France
Vengeoit l'honneur de ses premiers ayeux:

Lors qu'il tranchoit d'un bras victorieux
Au bord du Rhin l'Espagnolle vaillance,
Ja se traçant de l'aigu de sa lance
Un beau sentier pour s'en aller aux cieux.

Vous sainct troupeau, mon soustien et ma gloire,
Dont le beau vol m'a l'esprit enlevé,
Si autrefois m'avez permis de boire

Les eaux qui ont Hesiode abreuvé,
Soit pour jamais ce souspir engravé
Au plus sainct lieu du temple de Memoire.

CCXXIX

I went on pouring out all these tears,
In hope or distrust as it might chance,
When Henry, far from the borders of France,
Avenged the honor of his first forebears—

When with victorious arm, on the shores
Of the Rhine, he cut off the Spanish advance,
Already tracing at the point of his lance
A noble path to ascend to the stars.

You sacred troop, my sustenance and glory,
Whose noble flight has never let me sink,
If formerly you gave me leave to drink

The waters in which Hesiod was steeped,
May this sigh ever be engraved and kept
In the holiest part of the temple of Memory.[34]

---

34. The translation varies between iambic and anapestic tetrameter in the octave; the sestet is iambic pentameter except for the last line, which is anapestic tetrameter.

Line 1: The tears to which Ronsard refers are metaphorically the poems included in this first book of his love poems, the *Amours de Cassandre*. This poem marks the end of the first book.

3-8: The allusion is to Henry II's campaign against the Spanish in the spring of 1552. In line 8, I substitute "stars" for Ronsard's "cieux" (heavens).

9: An allusion to the Muses.

12: At the beginning of the *Theogony*, Hesiod refers to the Hippocrene, the fountain of the Muses on Mount Helicon.

14: Ronsard uses the adjective "sainct" (sacred, holy, or even saintly) in both line 9 and line 14.

Les Amours de Marie,
Le Deuxième Livre des Amours
II

Marie vous avez la joue aussi vermeille
Qu'une rose de May, vous avez les cheveux
Entre bruns et chatains, frisez de mille nœuds,
Gentement tortillez tout autour de l'oreille.

Quand vous estiez petite, une mignarde abeille
Sur vos lévres forma son nectar savoureux,
Amour laissa ses traits en vos yeux rigoureux,
Pithon vous feit la voix à nulle autre pareille.

Vous avez les tetins comme deux monts de lait,
Qui pommelent ainsi qu'au printemps nouvelet
Pommelent deux boutons que leur chasse environne,

De Junon sont vos bras, des Graces vostre sein,
Vous avez de l'Aurore et le front et la main,
Mais vous avez le cœur d'une fiere Lionne.

From *The Love Poems for Marie*

II

Vermillion are your cheeks, the same as are
Roses in May, Marie, and you have hair
Between light brown and chestnut red that swirls
Around your ears in pretty little curls.

When you were small a tiny bee perhaps
Formed its delicious nectar for your lips.
Love left his arrows in your two stern eyes,
And Peitho gave you the gift of an unmatched voice.

Each of your breasts is like a swelling mound
Of milk, just as in springtime can be found
Buds in their sheaths that swell like apples round.

Your arms are Juno's, your breasts come from the Graces,
Your rosy brow and hand Aurora's traces,
Your heart is like the fiercest lioness's.[1]

---

1. Line 8: Peitho is the goddess of persuasion. In Hesiod's *Theogony* she is one of the Okeanids (nymphs of the ocean).

13: Aurora is the goddess of the dawn.

IV

Le vingtiesme d'Avril couché sur l'herbelette,
Je vy ce me sembloit en dormant, un Chevreuil,
Qui çà qui là marchoit où le menoit son vueil,
Foulant les belles fleurs de mainte gambelette.

Une corne et une autre encore nouvelette
Enfloit son petit front d'un gracieux orgueil:
Comme un Soleil luisoit la rondeur de son œil,
Et un carquan pendoit sous sa gorge douillette.

Si tost que je le vy, je voulu courre apres,
Et lui qui m'avisa print sa fuite és forests,
Où se mocquant de moy ne me voulut attendre:

Mais en suivant son trac, je ne m'avisay pas
D'un piege entre les fleurs, qui me lia le pas:
Ainsi pour prendre autruy moy-mesme me fis prendre.

IV

The twentieth day of April, as on the grass I lay,
I saw within my sleep what seemed to be a deer,
Who, led by his desire, was ambling here and there,
Trampling the lovely flowers and gamboling in play.

One horn and then the other had newly sprouted; they
Swelled his little brow with graceful pride. The clear
Brightness of his round eye shone like the brightest star.
Beneath his downy throat a collar hung pearl-grey.

I wanted to chase after as soon as he came in sight,
But he, when he perceived me, into the woods took flight,
And seeming now to mock me, would not agree to stay.

But following his track, I failed to see the snare
Among the lovely flowers that seized upon me there.
Thus, trying to catch another, was caught myself that day.[2]

---

2. The translation is in iambic hexameter.

Line 2: I have translated Ronsard's "Chevreuil" in this case as a deer. More specifically, it is a roebuck.

V

Ce-pendant que tu vois le superbe rivage
De la riviere Tusque, et le mont Palatin,
Et que l'air des Latins te fait parler Latin,
Changeant à l'estranger ton naturel langage:

Une fille d'Anjou me detient en servage,
Ores baisant sa main et ores son tetin,
Et ores ses beaux yeux astres de mon destin.
Jy vy (comme l'on dit) trop plus heureux que sage.

Tu diras à Maigni, lisant ces vers ici,
C'est grand cas que Ronsard est encore amoureux!
Mon Bellay, je le suis, et le veux estre aussi,

Et ne veux confesser qu'amour soit malheureux,
Ou si c'est un malheur, baste, je delibere
De vivre malheureux en si belle misere.

V

While, you, for your part, are gazing upon
The Palatine hill and the proud Tiber's flow,
Changing your own tongue to a foreign one
As the Italian atmosphere makes you do,

I'm held in bondage by a girl of Anjou,
Now kissing her hand, now her beautiful eyes
(My destiny's stars), and her breasts now too,
Living, as one says, more happy than wise.

Reading these lines, you will say to Magny,
It's clear that Ronsard is in love once again!
Yes, I am, dear Bellay, and desire to be,

Nor want to admit that love is sheer pain;
Or, if it is, I resolve to remain
And inhabit this pain, this sweet misery.[3]

---

3. The translation varies between iambic and anapestic tetrameter. The poem is addressed to Joachim Du Bellay, who was in Italy at the time it was composed. Du Bellay's response to this poem can be found in sonnet 10 from his sequence *Les Regrets* (1558).

Line 2: The Palatine is the centermost of the Seven Hills of Rome. The Tiber is the river that runs through the city.

3: The line in the French ("Et que l'air des Latins te fait parler Latin") is somewhat ambiguous because "Latin" can mean "Roman" and hence "Italian," but during his sojourn in Italy Du Bellay wrote poems in Latin as well as in French.

5: Anjou is an historical province of France that straddles the Loire River (not to be confused with the Loir, which runs through Ronsard's town of Vendôme). Its capital is Angers.

9-12: Olivier de Magny (1529–1561), a poet and a disciple of Ronsard, was also in Italy at the time and was attached to Du Bellay.

VI

Douce belle amoureuse et bien-fleurante Rose,
Que tu es à bon droit aux amours consacrée!
Ta delicate odeur hommes et Dieux recrée,
Et bref, Rose tu es belle sur toute chose.

Marie pour son chef un beau bouquet compose
De ta fueille, et tousjours sa teste en est parée:
Tousjours ceste Angevine, unique Cytherée,
Du parfum de ton eau sa jeune face arrose.

Ha Dieu que je suis aise alors que je te voy
Esclorre au poinct du jour sur l'espine à requoy,
Aux jardins de Bourgueil pres d'une eau solitaire!

De toy les Nymphes ont les coudes et le sein,
De toy l'Aurore emprunte et sa joue et sa main,
Et son teint la beauté qu'on adore en Cythere.

VI

Fair-flowering Rose, sweet, lovely, amorous,
You signify love's power over us.
Both men and gods create your scent anew.
Nothing, in brief, is beautiful as you.

Marie makes fine bouquets to deck her hair
Out of your leaves—her head is never bare.
This Angevine, Cytherean in descent,
Washes her face in water that bears your scent.

God, when I see you on your thorn nearby
A solitary stream in the gardens of Bourgueil
Blooming at daybreak, I am filled with joy.

From you the Nymphs have rosy bosoms, and
From you Aurora gets her cheek and hand,
The beauteous tint adored in Venus's land.[4]

---

4. Line 7: "Angevine" is the feminine adjective of "Anjou," Marie's province. Cythera is an island sacred to Venus, so Ronsard's phrase points to how Marie is the descendant of Venus. In the French original, by a typical Ronsardian hyperbole, she is the only or especial descendant of Venus ("unique Cythérée").

11: Bourgueil is a commune in the Loire Valley noted for its vineyards.

14. Venus's land (in the translation) is the island of Cythera, which was sacred to her.

IX

Marie, qui voudroit vostre nom retourner,
Il trouveroit aimer: aimez-moy donc Marie,
Vostre nom de nature à l'amour vous convie.
À qui trahist Nature il ne faut pardonner.

S'il vous plaist vostre cœur pour gage me donner,
Je vous offre le mien: ainsi de ceste vie
Nous prendrons les plaisirs, et jamais autre envie
Ne me pourra l'esprit d'une autre emprisonner.

Il fault aimer, maistresse, au monde quelque chose.
Celuy qui n'aime point, malheureux se propose
Une vie de Scythe, et ses jours veut passer

Sans gouster la douceur des douceurs la meilleure.
Rien n'est doux sans Venus et sans son fils: à l'heure
Que je n'aimeray plus, puissé-je trespasser.

IX

Whoever wished to rearrange your name
Would find *aimer*: so love me, then, Marie.
Love calls you by your name—it's Nature's *aim*.
Traitors to Nature get no clemency.

Pledge me your heart and I will do the same
And offer mine: what pleasures there will be!
No other longings will have any claim
Or power upon my mind to imprison me.

Lady, one has to love something on earth.
Whoever doesn't lives a life that's worth
That of a Scythian, and his days are passed

Without tasting the best and sweetest taste.
Without Venus, nothing in life is sweet.
When mine lacks love, let me be done with it![5]

---

5. Lines 1-2: "Marie" is an anagram for "aimer" (to love), so I have retained the French.

11: The Scythians were Central-Asian nomads who seem to have been the first people to master warfare using bows-and-arrows on horseback. They are mentioned by Herodotus in the *Histories* and also in the New Testament Book of Colossians (3:11), where the term seems to be a metonymy for "barbarian."

X

Marie, en me tanceant vous me venez reprendre
Que je suis trop leger, et me dites tousjours,
Quand j'approche de vous, que j'aille à ma Cassandre,
Et tousjours m'appellez inconstant en amours.

« L'inconstance me plaist: les hommes sont bien lours,
« Qui de nouvelle amour ne se laissent surprendre:
Qui veult opiniastre une seule pretendre
N'est digne que Venus luy face de bons tours.

Celuy qui n'ose faire une amitié nouvelle,
A faute de courage, ou faute de cervelle,
Se défiant de soy que ne peut avoir mieux.

Les hommes maladifs ou mattez de vieillesse
Doivent estre constans: mais sotte est la jeunesse,
Qui n'est point esveillée et qui n'aime en cent lieux.

X

You scold me, Marie, and take me to task
For being too fickle, and frequently ask
Why I don't go back to Cassandra, and then
You call me inconstant in love once again.

"Inconstancy pleases me: dull is the man
Who will not embrace a new love if he can,"
But stubbornly cleaves to one mistress. He earns
No favors from Venus, the goddess he spurns.

Someone too timid or fearful to start
New friendships, for want of brains or of heart,
His lack of assurance is all he embraces.

Men who are sickly or agèd or both—
They have to be constant; but foolish is youth
Who doesn't find love in a hundred places.[6]

---

6. This is an irregular sonnet in the French. Almost all of Ronsard's sonnets take the Petrarchan form, with a rhyme scheme of *abba abba* in the octave. Here the rhyme scheme in the French is *abab baab*. The translation varies between iambic and anapestic tetrameter.

Lines 5-6: These lines are enclosed in quotation marks, perhaps to indicate that this is Ronsard's usual reply to Marie's complaint of his inconstancy.

XIV

Amour, quiconque ait dit que le ciel fut ton pere,
Et que la Cyprienne en ses flancs te porta,
Il trompa les humains, un Dieu ne t'enfanta:
Tu n'es pas fils du ciel, Venus n'est pas ta mere.

Des champs Massyliens la plus cruelle Fere
Entre ses lionneaux dans un roc t'alaitta,
Et t'ouvrant ses tetins par son laict te jetta
Tout à l'entour du cœur sa rage la plus fiere.

Rien ne te plaist, cruel, que sanglots et que pleurs,
Que deschirer nos cœurs d'espineuses douleurs,
Que tirer tout d'un coup mille morts de ta trousse.

Un si meschant que toy du ciel n'est point venu:
Si Venus t'eust conceu tu eusses retenu
Quelque peu de douceur d'une mere si douce.

XIV

Amor, whoever called the sky your father,
And said the Cyprian bore you in her womb,
Deceived us: from a god you did not come;
You aren't heaven's offspring; Venus is not your mother.

The cruelest beast of the Massilian fields of war
Suckled you in a rock between her young,
And with her breast-milk hurled you out headlong
From the heart of her most fierce anger, everywhere.

Cruel, you're pleased by naught but sobs and tears
That harrow our hearts with sorrow's piercing briars,
As you draw myriad death-blows from your quiver.

From heaven such a wicked one came never.
Had Venus borne you, you'd have still retained
Some kindness from a mother so very kind.[7]

---

7. Line 1: Hesiod in the *Theogony* sees Eros (the Greek name for Amor) as being one of the first of things and as having sprung from Chaos. In later myths, he is the offspring of Aphrodite (Venus), the goddess of love and beauty, and Ares (Mars), the god of war. In some stories, however, Eros is the son of Aphrodite and Zeus (Jupiter), the sky god.

2: The Cyprian is Venus (by metonymy); the island of Cyprus was sacred to her.

5: A reference to the siege and naval battle of Massilia (the Roman name for Marseille), fought in 49 B.C. as part of Caesar's civil war.

XIX

Marie levez-vous ma jeune paresseuse,
Ja la gaye Alouette au ciel a fredonné,
Et ja le rossignol doucement jargonné
Dessus l'espine assis sa complainte amoureuse.

Sus debout allon voir l'herbelette perleuse,
Et vostre beau rosier de boutons couronné,
Et vos œillets mignons ausquels aviez donné
Hier au soir de l'eau d'une main si songneuse.

Harsoir en vous couchant vous jurastes vos yeux
D'estre plus-tost que moy ce matin esveillée:
Mais le dormir de l'Aube aux filles gracieux

Vous tient d'un doux sommeil encor les yeux sillée.
Ça ça que jes les baise et vostre beau tetin
Cent fois pour vous apprendre à vous lever matin.

XIX

Get up, Marie, my sweet, young lazybones:
The Lark's already trilling to the sky;
Already now the Nightingale intones,
Perched on a thorn, its lovesick melody.

Let's go and see the grass all pearled with dew,
Your lovely rosebush crowned with blossoms, and
Those fine carnations which last evening you
Carefully watered with attentive hand.

You swore to me by your own eyes last night
To be awake before me at the prime;
But the sleep of Dawn, which gives girls such delight,

Sealing your eyes, still holds you in sweet rest.
I'll kiss them many times, and your soft breast,
To teach you to get out of bed on time.

XXVIII

Vous mesprisez nature: estes-vous si cruelle
De ne vouloir aimer? voyez les Passereaux
Qui demenent l'amour, voyez les Colombeaux,
Regardez le Ramier, voyez la Tourterelle:

Voyez deçà delà d'une fretillante aile
Voleter par les bois les amoureux oiseaux,
Voyez la jeune vigne embrasser les ormeaux,
Et toute chose rire en la saison nouvelle.

Ici la bergerette en tournant son fuseau
Desgoise ses amours, et là le pastoureau
Respond à sa chanson, ici toute chose aime:

Tout parle de l'amour, tout s'en veut enflamer:
Seulement vostre cœur froid d'une glace extreme
Demeure opiniastre et ne veut point aimer.

XXVIII

Are you so cruel as not to want to love?
Is it contempt for Nature? See the sparrow:
The urge to love has stirred him to the marrow;
Behold the ringdove and the turtledove.

See how the amorous birds on quivering wing
Are fluttering here and there from bough to bough:
The young vine curls around the elm trees now:
All things are filled with laughter in the spring.

The shepherdess, turning her spindle, sings
Her loves; the shepherd tunes his melody
To answer her, for love is in all things.

All speak of love, all enter in its fire:
Only your heart, as cold as it can be,
Stays obstinate and still disdains desire.[8]

---

8. Line 3: The phrase "to the marrow" is my interpolation.

XXIX

J'aime la fleur de Mars, j'aime la belle rose,
L'une qui est sacrée à Venus la Deesse,
L'autre qui a le nom de ma belle maistresse,
Pour qui troublé d'esprit en paix je ne repose.

J'aime trois oiselets, l'un qui sa plume arrose
De la pluye de May, et vers le Ciel se dresse:
L'autre qui veuf au bois lamente sa destresse:
L'autre qui pour son fils mille versets compose.

J'aime un pin de Bourgeuil, où Venus apendit
Ma jeune liberté, quand prise elle rendit
Mon cœur que doucement un bel œil emprisonne.

J'aime un jeune laurier de Phœbus l'arbrisseau,
Dont ma belle maistresse en pliant un rameau
Lié de ses cheveux me fist une couronne.

XXIX

I love the violet and the lovely rose:
The first one sacred to the goddess Venus,
The other with the name of my fair mistress,
Because of whom I never have repose.

I love three little birds: first is the one
Who lifts wet feathers skyward after spring rains,
Then one who, widowed, to the wood complains,
One who composes verses for her dead son.

I love a Burgundian pine where Venus hung
My youthful liberty when, being enraptured,
It yielded up my heart an eye had captured.

I love a young laurel, Phoebus Apollo's tree,
From which my mistress took a branch and strung
With plaits of her own hair a crown for me.[9]

---

9. Lines 1-2: Ronsard's phrase "fleur de Mars" (flower of March) in the French refers to the violet. He claims in various poems that the violet is sacred to Venus; see, for example, Ode XXXVIII (Pléiade edition, 1.841).

5-8: The three birds, respectively, are the lark, the turtledove, and the nightingale. The turtledove is renowned for fidelity. In Book 19 of the *Odyssey*, the story is told of Aëdon, who, envying her sister Niobe, the mother of six sons and six daughters, tries to murder Sipylus, the eldest of them, but ends up killing her own son, Itylus, by mistake and is transformed by Zeus to a nightingale.

9: The Burgundian pine is probably an allusion to Marie; her surname was "Du Pin" or "Dupin."

12: For the connection between Apollo and the laurel, see the note to line 14 of Sonnet CLXV of *The Love Poems for Cassandra* above.

XXXI

S'il y a quelque fille en toute une contrée,
Qui soit inexorable, inhumaine et cruelle,
Tousjours elle est de moy pour dame rencontrée,
Et tousjours le malheur me fait serviteur d'elle.

Mais si quelcune est douce honneste aimable et belle,
La prinse en est pour moy tousjours desesperée:
J'ay beau estre courtois jeune accort et fidelle,
Elle sera tousjours d'un sot enamourée.

Sous tel astre malin je nasquis en ce monde!
« Voyla que c'est d'aimer: ceux qui ont merité
« D'estre recompensez sont en douleur profonde:

« Et le sot volontiers est tousjours bien traité.
« Ô traistre et lasche Amour que tu es malheureux!
« Malheureux est celuy qui devient amoureux.

XXXI

If in an entire country there should be
A girl who's cruel, obdurate, inhuman,
The one I always fasten on is she:
I always dance attendance on that woman.

But if she's pleasant, honest, lovely, sweet,
Making her mine is hopeless, as a rule;
In vain might I be faithful, young, discreet,
She'll always be enamored of a fool.

What wicked star presided at my birth!
"See how it is to love: those who are worth
Being recompensed are very deeply pained,

While the willful fool is always well entertained.
O treacherous Love, unfortunate that you are,
The lover is more unfortunate by far."[10]

---

10. As with Sonnet X of *The Love Poems for Marie* above above, this is an irregular sonnet; its rhyme scheme is *abab baba* in the octave.

Lines 10-14: Ronsard's scare quotes suggest either that the assertion he is making in these lines is proverbial or that he is framing them as proverbial.

XLIV

Marie, baisez-moy: non, ne me baisez pas,
Mais tirez moy le cœur de vostre douce haleine:
Non, ne le tirez pas, mais hors de chaque veine
Succez-moy toute l'ame esparse entre vos bras:

Non, ne la succez pas: car apres le trespas
Que serois-je sinon une semblance vaine,
Sans corps desur la rive, où l'amour ne demeine
(Pardonne moy Pluton) qu'en feintes ses esbas?

Pendant que nous vivons, entr'aimons nous, Marie,
Amour ne regne point sur la troupe blesmie
Des morts, qui sont sillez d'un long somme de fer.

C'est abus que Pluton ait aimé Proserpine,
Si doux soing n'entre point en si dure poitrine:
Amour regne en la terre et non point en enfer.

XLIV

Kiss me, Marie—or no, don't kiss me, then,
But draw out my heart with your sweet breath; or no,
Suck out my soul instead from every vein:
Between your arms release it, let it flow.

No, do not suck it out; for, should it go,
What but a bodiless phantom would remain—
Upon that shore where love can only feign
(Pardon me, Pluto) joys it cannot know?

Let's love each other while we live, Marie:
Love doesn't reign over the pallid legions
Of those whose eyes are sealed in ironbound rest.

That Pluto loved Proserpina's a lie;
For such sweet pain can't pierce so hard a breast:
Love reigns on earth, not in the infernal regions.[11]

---

11. Lines 8-12: Pluto (the Roman name for Hades) is the king of the Underworld, and Proserpina (the Roman name for Persephone) is its queen. Proserpina was abducted by Pluto (in some stories, with the connivance of Jupiter), but when her mother Ceres (Demeter), the goddess of the grain, threatened to withhold fertility, Jupiter arranged to have Proserpina live with Pluto during the winter months and with Ceres during the rest of the year.

LXIII

Que dis-tu, que fais-tu pensive Tourterelle
Dessus cest arbre sec?   T.   Viateur, je lamente.
R.   Pourquoi lamentes-tu ?   T.   Pour ma compagne absente,
Dont je meurs de douleur.   R..   En quelle part est-elle ?

T.   Un cruel oiseleur par glueuse cautelle
L'a prise et l'a tuée: et nuict et jour je chante
Ses obseques ici, nommant la mort mechante
Qu'elle ne m'a tuée avecques ma fidelle.

R.   Voudrois-tu bien mourir et suivre ta compagne?
T.   Aussi bien je languis en ce bois tenebreux,
Où tousjours le regret de sa mort m'accompagne.

R..   Ô gentils oiselets que vous estes heureux!
Nature elle mesme à l'amour vous enseigne,
Qui vivez et mourez fideles amoureux.

LXIII

What are you doing, pensive turtledove,
On that dry branch?　T.　Wayfarer, as you see,
I'm grieving.　R.　Why?　T.　Because of my absent love,
For whom I die of sadness.　R.　Where is she?

T.　A cruel birder caught her with crafty lime
And killed her; so I constantly intone
Her obsequies, while blaming death that I'm
Still living and without my faithful one.

R.　And would you follow after her if you could?
T.　That's why I languish in this gloomy wood,
Always accompanied by my grief for her.

R.　O gentle little birds, how blessed you are!
Nature's instruction binds you to her will,
Who live and die as faithful lovers still.[12]

---

12. This sonnet takes the form of a dialogue between Ronsard (R) and the turtledove (Tourterelle—T). The turtledove is renowned for its fidelity.

LXVI

Je mourrois de plaisir voyant par ces bocages
Les arbres enlacez de lierres espars,
Et la verde lambrunche errante en mille pars
Sur l'aubespin fleury pres des roses sauvages.

Je mourrois de plaisir oyant les doux ramages
Des Hupes, des Coqus, et des Ramiers rouhars
Dessur un arbre verd bec en bec fretillars,
Et des Tourtres aux bois voyant les mariages.

Je mourrois de plaisir voyant en ces beaux mois
Debusquer au matin le Chevreuil hors du bois,
Et de voir fretiller dans le Ciel l'Alouette :

Je mourrois de plaisir où je languis transi
Absent de la beauté qu'en ce pré je souhaite.
« Un demy jour d'absence est un an de souci.

LXVI

I'd die of pleasure seeing throughout this grove
Ivy's profusion twining the trees with love,
And the green grapevine—everywhere it roams
Over the hawthorn, near where the wild rose blooms.

I'd die of pleasure hearing the warbling too
Of hoopoes and woodcocks, ringdoves that bill and coo,
Their twittering beaks aflutter on green tree-tops,
And seeing the turtledoves mating in a copse.

I'd die of pleasure seeing in this fine spring
The roebuck stirring out of the woods at dawn
And in the heavens the lark frisking its wing.

I'd die of pleasure where, benumbed, I languish,
The beauty for which I'm always yearning gone.
"A half-day's absence is a year of anguish."[13]

---

13. Line 14: The quotation marks indicate that the thought is proverbial.

LXVII

En vain pour vous ce bouquet je compose,
En vain pour vous ma Deesse il est fait:
Vostre beauté est bouquet du bouquet,
La fleur des fleurs la rose de la rose.

Vous et les fleurs differez d'une chose,
C'est que l'Hyver les fleurettes desfait,
Vostre Printemps en ses graces parfait
Ne craint des ans nulle metamorphose.

Heureux bouquet, n'entre point au sejour
De ce beau sein, ce beau logis d'Amour,
Ne touche point ceste pomme jumelle:

Ton lustre gay d'ardeur se faniroit,
Et ta verdeur sans grace periroit,
Comme je suis fany pour l'amour d'elle.

LXVII

For you, in vain, this garland I compose,
For you, in vain, my Goddess, is it made:
Your beauty is its own best accolade,
The flower of flowers, the quintessential rose.

The one way that you differ from all those
Flowers is that in winter they're unmade:
Your spring of perfect bloom is not afraid
Of any changes that the years impose.

Happy bouquet, you should not ever come
To this fair breast, where Love has made its home,
Or touch the twin ripe apples that are there.

Your brilliant luster would soon fade away,
Your freshness wither, subject to decay,
As I have withered out of love for her.

LXVIII

Cesse tes pleurs, mon livre: il n'est pas ordonné
Du destin, que moy vif tu sois riche de gloire:
Avant que l'homme passe outre la rive noire,
L'honneur de son travail ne luy est point donné.

Quelqu'un apres mille ans de mes vers estonné
Voudra dans mon Loir, comme en Permesse, boire:
Et voyant mon pays, à peine pourra croire
Que d'un si petit lieu tel Poëte soit né.

« Pren, mon livre, pren cœur: la vertu precieuse
« De l'homme, quand il vit, est tousjours odieuse:
« Apres qu'il est absent, chacun le pense un Dieu.

« La rancœur nuit tousjours à ceux qui sont en vie:
« Sur les vertus d'un mort elle n'a plus de lieu,
« Et la posterité rend l'honneur sans envie.

LXVIII

Stop grieving, my book, that you're still without fame,
And while I am living your stock doesn't soar:
Until a man passes beyond the black shore,
The honor he's earned isn't given to him.

In hundreds of years, those my verses enflame,
As in the Permessus, will drink in my Loir,
And seeing my country, will wonder the more
That so paltry a place such a poet can claim.

A man's great attainments are never thought good
In his lifetime, my book, so take heart, come what may:
After he's gone, he's revered as a god.

Over only the living does malice hold sway:
On a dead man's virtues it doesn't have force.
Posterity honors his deeds in due course.[14]

---

14. The translation varies between iambic and anapestic tetrameter. Ronsard's note indicates that this poem marks the end of the first part of the *Amours* of Marie.

5: More literally: 'Someone, after a thousand years, amazed by my verses . . ."

6: The Permessus is a stream on Mount Helicon, the mountain where the Muses live; hence, to drink from the Permessus is to take inspiration.

7: "Country" (pays) has the sense here of region or locale.

9-14: The entire sestet is in quotation marks in the French text. Evidently, Ronsard is paraphrasing ideas he considers proverbial.

14: More literally: "And posterity renders him honor without envy."

Sur La Mort de Marie

I

Je songeois sous l'obscur de la nuict endormie,
Qu'un sepulchre entre-ouvert s'apparoissoit à moy:
La Mort gisoit dedans toute palle d'effroy,
Dessus estoit escrit Le tombeau de Marie.

Espovanté du songe en sursault je m'escrie,
Amour est donc sujet à nostre humaine loy!
Il a perdu son regne, et le meilleur de soy,
Puis que par une mort sa puissance est perie.

Je n'avois achevé, qu'au poinct du jour voicy
Un Passant à ma porte adeulé de soucy,
Qui de la triste mort m'annonça la nouvelle.

Pren courage mon ame, il faut suivre sa fin,
Je l'entens dans le ciel comme elle nous appelle:
Mes pieds avec les siens ont fait mesme chemin.

On the Death of Marie

I

I dreamt in the darkness of the sleeping night
That a half-open grave appeared to me:
Death lay within, all pale with fright,
And above was written, "The Tomb of Marie."

Appalled by that dream, with a start I cried,
Then Love is subject to Mortality!
Since by a death his power has died,
He has lost his reign and his identity.

I had not yet finished when, at break of day,
A care-worn passerby at my door
Gave me the news that she had passed away.

Take courage, my soul: we have to follow her.
I hear her in the heavens as if calling us there:
My feet after hers have taken the same way.[15]

---

15. The translation varies between iambic and anapestic tetrameter and pentameter. For a brief discussion of the poems in the "On the Death of Marie" sequence, see the Introduction.

Line 14: Literally: "My feet with hers have taken the same path." By substituting "after" for "with," I am normalizing Ronsard's grammar. Clearly, prolepsis is operating here, but the conception is somewhat opaque.

II

Terre ouvre moy ton sein, et me laisse reprendre
Mon thresor, que la Parque a caché dessous toy:
Ou bien si tu ne peux, ô terre cache moy
Sous mesme sepulture avec sa belle cendre.

Le traict qui la tua, devoit faire descendre
Mon corps aupres du sien pour finir mon esmoy:
Aussi bien, veu le mal qu'en sa mort je reçoy,
Je ne sçaurois plus vivre, et me fasche d'attendre.

Quand ses yeux m'esclairoient, et qu'en terre j'avois
Le bon-heur de les voir, à l'heure je vivois,
Ayant de leurs rayons mon ame gouvernee,

Maintenant je suis mort: la Mort qui s'en alla
Loger dedans ses yeux, en partant m'appella,
Et me fit de son soir accomplir ma journee.

II

Open your bosom, Earth, and render me
My treasure, which was hidden in you by Fate,
Or if you can't, then hide me, Earth, in that
Same sepulcher wherein her ashes lie.

The shaft that killed her should have made me die,
Ending thereby this agonizing state
In which the pain her death caused won't abate:
I do not live, am raging inwardly.

For when her eyes shone on me and I had
The happiness to see them, then I led
A vibrant life, my soul ruled by their rays.

Now I am dead: for Death which since has gone
To live within her eyes calls me anon,
Urging me from her night to end my days.[16]

---

16. Line 2: Ronsard's name for fate in this instance is "la Parque." The *Parcae* (Latin) are the Three Fates and are equivalent to the *Moirai* of Greek mythology.

III

Alors que plus amour nourrissoit mon ardeur,
M'asseurant de jouyr de ma longue esperance:
À l'heure que j'avois en luy plus d'asseurance,
La Mort a moissoné mon bien en sa verdeur.

J'esperois par souspirs, par peine, et par langueur
Adoucir son orgueil: las! je meurs quand j'y pense,
Mais en lieu d'en jouyr, pour toute recompense
Un cercueil tient enclos mon espoir et mon cœur.

Je suis bien malheureux, puis qu'elle vive et morte
Ne me donne repos, et que de jour en jour
Je sens par son trespas une douleur plus forte.

Comme elle je devrois reposer à mon tour:
Toutesfois je ne voy par quel chemin je sorte,
Tant la Mort me rempestre au labyrinth d'amour.

III

Making me think my hopes would be fulfilled,
Love fed my ardor—it was never stilled;
And when he had gained my confidence, just then,
Death harvested my fruit, though it was green.

I'd hoped my painful sighs could mollify
His arrogance—that memory makes me die!
In place of joy, alas, with each new thought
A coffin binds my hopes up and my heart.

Unhappy that I am I've found no peace—
Not since she's dead or when she was alive—
And day by day I feel my woes increase.

Like her I ought to find repose in death,
But nowhere that I turn reveals the path:
Death tangles me in labyrinths of love.

IV

Comme on voit sur la branche au mois de May la rose
En sa belle jeunesse, en sa premiere fleur,
Rendre le ciel jaloux de sa vive couleur,
Quand l'Aube de ses pleurs au poinct du jour l'arrose:

La grace dans sa fueille, et l'amour se repose,
Embasmant les jardins et les arbres d'odeur:
Mais batue ou de pluye, ou d'excessive ardeur,
Languissante elle meurt fueille à fueille déclose.

Ainsi en ta premiere et jeune nouveauté,
Quand la terre et le ciel honoroient ta beauté,
La Parque t'a tuee, et cendre tu reposes.

Pour obseques reçoy mes larmes et mes pleurs,
Ce vase plein de laict, ce panier plein de fleurs,
Afin que vif et mort ton corps ne soit que roses.

IV

Just as one sees the rose on its stem in May,
In youthful beauty, in its earliest flower,
Making sky jealous of its vibrant color,
By Dawn's tears watered at the break of day:

Grace in each fold and love in full display,
Embalming the gardens and the trees with odor;
But beaten by rain or by excessive ardor,
Languish and die, till fold upon fold falls away:

So in the earliest newness of your youth,
Your beauty honored both by heaven and earth,
Fate cut you off, and now your dust reposes.

For obsequy, receive from me these tears,
This bowl of milk, this basket full of flowers,
So that alive and dead you are naught but roses.[17]

---

17. Line 11: Here again, as in the second of the sonnets "On the Death of Marie," Ronsard's name for fate is "la Parque."

Le Premier Livre des Sonnets pour Hélène

III

Ma douce Helene, non, mais bien ma douce haleine,
Qui froide rafraischis la chaleur de mon cœur,
Je prens de ta vertu cognoissance et vigueur,
Et ton œil comme il veut à son plaisir me meine.

Heureux celuy qui souffre une amoureuse peine
Pour un nom si fatal: heureuse la douleur,
Bien-heureux le torment, qui vient pour la valeur
Des yeux, non pas des yeux, mais l'astre d'Helene.

Nom, malheur des Troyens, sujet de mon souci,
Ma sage Penelope et mon Helene aussi,
Qui d'un soin amoureux tout le cœur m'envelope:

Nom, qui m'a jusqu'au ciel de la terre enlevé,
Qui eust jamais pensé que j'eusse retrouvé
En une mesme Helene une autre Penelope?

From *The First Book of Sonnets for Hélène*

III

Sweet Helen, breath of life, my sweet *haleine*,
Warming my heart through your reviving chill,
I draw from your strength and knowledge and remain
Drawn by the eyes that lead me where they will.

Happy is he who suffers a lover's pain
For a name so fateful; happy is his ordeal:
Blessèd the grief of one whose hope is still
To gain not just the eyes but the star of Hélène.

Name, bane of the Trojans, subject of my woe,
My sage Penelope and my Helen too,
Enveloping me in love's anxiety:

Name, which has elevated me to heaven,
Who would have ever thought that I'd be given
In the same Helen a Penelope?[1]

---

1. Line 1: Ronsard is punning on Hélène's name in that "haleine" in French means "breath." The Greek etymology of the name has been much debated. To keep the pun, I have retained the French word but have interpolated the phrase "breath of life." The literal meaning of line 1 is, "My sweet Hélène, no, but really my sweet breath."

6: The poet interprets the Helen of the *Iliad*—whom he makes parallel to his own Hélène—as embodying and personifying the fateful (and fatal) power of Eros. ("Fatal" in the French can have both meanings.)

9-14: Ronsard is here conflating the antithetical figures of Helen, whose act of eloping with Paris precipitated the Trojan War, and Penelope, who remained faithful to Odysseus.

VI

Dedans les flots d'Amour je n'ay point de support,
Je ne voy point de Phare, et si je ne desire
(Ô desir trop hardy!) sinon que ma Navire
Apres tant de perils puisse gaigner le port.

Las! devant que payer mes vœux dessus le bort,
Naufrage je mourray: car je ne voy reluire
Qu'une flame sur moy, qu'une Helene qui tire
Entre mille rochers ma Navire à la mort.

Je suis seul me noyant de ma vie homicide,
Choisissant un enfant un aveugle pour guide,
Dont il me faut de honte et pleurer et rougir.

Je ne sçay si mes sens ou si ma raison tasche
De conduire ma nef: mais je sçay qu'il me fasche
De voir un si beau port et n'y pouvoir surgir.

VI

Amidst Love's rolling tides I've no support:
I see no Beacon, and my sole desire—
Desire too bold!—is that the Ship I steer,
After such perils, will have gained a port.

Shipwrecked, I'll perish, never more draw breath,
Before I've reached the shore and made my vows:
One light shines over me, one Helen draws
My Ship among the rocks to certain death.

Drowning in solitude, a suicide,
I've chosen a blind infant as my guide,
For which I weep and blush in my chagrin.

Whether my senses or my reason strive
To steer my boat, yet still it makes me grieve
To see a port I cannot enter in.[2]

---

2. Lines 7-8: In line with his interpretation of Homer's Helen as embodying and personifying the fateful (and fatal) power of Eros, Ronsard's Hélène is the star that draws his ship to death among the rocks.

VII

Amour abandonnant les vergers de Cytheres,
D'Amathonte et d'Eryce, en la France passa:
Et me monstrant son arc, comme Dieu, me tança,
Que j'oubliois, ingrat, ses loix et ses mysteres.

Il me frappa trois fois de ses ailes legeres:
Un traict le plus aigu dans les yeux m'eslança.
La playe vint au cœur, qui chaude me laissa
Une ardeur de chanter les honneurs de Surgeres.

Chante (me dist Amour) sa grace et sa beauté
Sa bouche ses beaux yeux sa douceur sa bonté:
Je la garde pour toy le sujet de ta plume.

Un sujet si divin ma Muse ne poursuit.
Je te feray l'esprit meilleur que de coustume:
« L'homme ne peut faillir, quand un Dieu le conduit.

VII

Leaving the Cyprian groves and Sicily's
And Cythera's behind, Love went to France,
And showing his bow with angry countenance,
Said I'd forgotten his laws and mysteries.

Three times he struck me with his wings, and then
Into my eyes his keenest arrow shot.
The wound went to my heart: it left me hot,
Ardent to sing the praises of Hélène.

Sing (then said Love) her beauty and her grace,
Her mouth, her lovely eyes, her gentleness:
I have reserved her for you as your theme.

So high a theme my Muse has not pursued.
To elevate your spirit is my aim:
"Man cannot fail when guided by a God."[3]

---

3. Lines 1-2: Cyprus, Sicily, and Cythera were all said to be sacred to Venus.

8: More literally: ". . . the honors of Surgères," which was Hélène's surname.

9-14: Love speaks in lines 9-11. Ronsard answers in line 12. Love responds in line 13. The fact that line 14 is in quotation marks again indicates that it expresses a proverbial idea.

IX

L'autre jour que j'estois sur le haut d'un degré,
Passant tu m'advisas, et me tournant la veue,
Tu m'esblouïs les yeux, tant j'avois l'ame esmeue
De me voir en sursaut de tes yeux rencontré.

Ton regard dans le cœur, dans le sang m'est entré
Comme un esclat de foudre alors qu'il fend la nue:
J'euz de froid et de chaud la fiévre continue,
D'un si poignant regard mortellement outré.

Lors si ta belle main passant ne m'eust fait signe,
Main blanche, qui se vante estre fille d'un Cygne,
Je fusse mort, Helene, aux rayons de tes yeux:

Mais ton signe retint l'ame presque ravie,
Ton œil se contenta d'estre victorieux,
Ta main se resjouyt de me donner la vie.

IX

The other day I stood atop a stair
As you passed by: your gaze caught mine; your eyes
Dazzled my own, so great was my surprise,
So deeply was I moved to see you there.

Your gaze cut through my spirit in a blaze,
Just as a lightning bolt will cleave a cloud;
Continually feverish, I turned hot and cold,
Mortally wounded by your piercing gaze.

Then, if your white hand hadn't made a sign
In passing, vaunted daughter of the Swan,
I would have died, Hélène, from your eyes' bright rays.

My almost ravished soul was rescued thus:
Your eye was pleased to be victorious,
But your hand rejoiced at lengthening my days.[4]

---

4. Lines 9-11: Helen of Troy was the daughter of Zeus, who took the form of a Swan in his rape of Leda. The end-rhymes of lines 9 and 10 ("sign" and "Swan") are the homophones "signe" and "Cygne" in the French. Ronsard makes symbolic use of the same homophones in the last of his *Derniers vers*.

14: Literally: "at giving me life."

XXII

Puis qu'elle est tout hyver, toute la mesme glace,
Toute neige, et son cœur tout armé de glaçons,
Qui ne m'aime sinon pour avoir mes chansons,
Pourquoy suis-je si fol que je ne m'en delace?

Dequoy me sert son nom, sa grandeur et sa race,
Que d'honneste servage et de belles prisons?
Maistresse, je n'ay pas les cheveux si grisons,
Qu'une autre de bon cœur ne prenne vostre place.

Amour, qui est enfant, ne cele verité.
Vous n'estes si superbe, ou si riche en beauté,
Qu'il faille desdaigner un bon cœur qui vous aime.

R'entrer en mon Avril desormais je ne puis:
Aimez moy, s'il vous plaist, grison comme je suis,
Et je vous aimeray quand vous serez de mesme.

XXII

Because she is all winter, snow and ice,
And icicles around her heart have grown,
And only loves me for my songs alone,
Why am I bound to her as in a vise?

What good to me her name, her grandeur, race,
But servitude, fair-seeming slavery!
Mistress, my hair is not as yet so gray
That no one would be glad to take your place.

Love, being an infant, never hides the truth:
You aren't so grand or in such perfect youth
That you can treat a good heart with such scorn.

Though I can't make my April days return,
Love me, I beg you, gray-haired as I am,
And I will love you when you are the same.[5]

---

5. Line 4: The phrase "as in a vise" is an interpolation: Ronsard's wording ("que je m'en delace") means: "that I cannot disentangle myself from her."

XXVI

Je fuy les pas frayez du meschant populaire,
Et les villes où sont les peuples amassez:
Les rochers, les forests desja sçavent assez
Quelle trampe a ma vie estrange et solitaire.

Si ne suis-je si seul, qu'Amour mon secretaire
N'accompagne mes pieds debiles et cassez:
Qu'il ne conte mes maux et presens et passez
À ceste voix sans corps, qui rien ne sçauroit taire.

Souvent plein de discours, pour flatter mon esmoy,
Je m'arreste, et je dy, Se pourroit-il bien faire
Qu'elle pensast, parlast, ou se souvint de moy?

Qu'à sa pitié mon mal commençast à desplaire?
Encor que je me trompe, abusé du contraire,
Pour me faire plaisir, Helene, je le croy.

XXVI

I flee the beaten paths of the populace
And the towns where the vicious gather *en masse*:
The rocks and the forests—they know well indeed
How strange and lonely is this life I lead:

So lonely that my sole companion, Love,
Follows my faltering steps at no remove,
Telling my past and present grievances
To this bodiless voice that nothing silences.

Filled up with speech and to soothe my emotion,
I stop and I say: could it possibly be
That she thinks, speaks, or has memories of me—

Or has she lost interest in pitying my grief?
I flatter myself with the contrary notion.
To make myself happy I cling to belief.[6]

---

6. The translation varies between iambic pentameter and anapestic tetrameter.

Lines 8-9: The editors of the Pléiade gloss "this bodiless voice" ("ceste voix sans corps") as "the voice of Echo" (in the myth of Echo and Narcissus; see 1.1370). This is plausible, but I think that Ronsard may also be referring to the voice of his own poetry, which confronts him as a kind of phantom presence outside himself.

12: Literally: "That pitying my suffering begins to displease her."

XXVII

Chef, escole des arts, le sejour de science,
Où vit un intellect qui foy du Ciel nous fait,
Une heureuse memoire, un jugement parfait,
D'où Pallas reprendroit sa seconde naissance.

Chef, le logis d'honneur, de vertu, de prudence,
Ennemy capital du vice contrefait:
Chef, petit Univers, qui montres par effet
Que tu as du grand Tour parfaite cognoissance:

Et toy divin Esprit qui du Ciel és venu,
En son chef comme au Ciel sainctement retenu
Simple rond et parfait, comme icy nous ne sommes.

Où tout est embrouillé, sans ordre ny sans loy,
Puisque tu es divin, ayes pitié de moy:
Il appartient aux Dieux d'avoir pitié des hommes.

XXVII

Head, school of the arts and science's domain,
Where intellect lives and gives us faith in Heaven,
A happy memory, perfect judgment even,
And from which Pallas Athena is born again.

Head, lodge of honor, virtue, prudence—bane
Of all dissembling vice and what is craven;
A universe in small, to which is given
The power to comprehend and to explain.

And you, divine Spirit, from Heaven ordained,
At its height as in Heaven by holiness retained,
Simple, round, perfect, as here we are not—

Where all is embroiled, without harmony:
As you are divine, have pity on me.
It pertains to the Gods to pity man's lot.[7]

---

7. The translation varies between iambic pentameter and anapestic tetrameter.

Line 4: The goddess Athena (the Roman Minerva) was born out of the head of Zeus (Jupiter) and is associated with wisdom. Her epithet "Pallas" is of uncertain meaning. Ronsard's syncretism—the way he brings together the pagan Athena and Christian faith—is very much in evidence here.

6: The phrase "and what is craven" is my interpolation.

7-8: The "universe in small" ("petit Univers") is a reference to the Neoplatonist idea of the mind as a microcosm of all things. This idea is more clearly presented in line 8 of the original: "Que tu as du grand Tout parfait cognoissance" ("That you have perfect understanding of the grand Totality [of things]").

9-14: The sestet turns from the mind to the spirit, which in the conception developed here is at once embodied in the individual and yet separate from him or her in that it emanates from the godhead. Consequently, in Ronsard's conception, though the world is "embroiled, without harmony" ("embrouillé, sans ordre ny sans loi"), we are able to intuit an untrammeled perfection.

XXXIII

Nous promenant tous seuls, vous me distes, Maistresse,
Qu'un chant vous desplaisoit, s'il estoit doucereux:
Que vous aimiez les plaints des tristes amoureux,
Toute voix lamentable et pleine de tristesse.

Et pource (disiez-vous) quand je suis loin de presse,
Je choisis vos Sonnets qui sont plus douloureux:
Puis d'un chant qui est propre au sujet langoureus,
Ma nature et Amour veulent que je me paisse.

Vos propos sont trompeurs. Si vous aviez souci
De ceux qui ont un cœur larmoyant et transi,
Je vous ferois pitié par une sympathie:

Mais vostre œil cauteleux, trop finement subtil,
Pleure en chantant mes vers, comme le Crocodil,
Pour mieux me desrober par feintise la vie.

XXXIII

You said to me, Mistress, as we walked alone,
You aren't pleased by songs that are sugared; instead
You like the plaints of lovers that are sad,
All lamentations in a doleful tone.

When I am far from people (so you said),
I choose your Sonnets that seem most to mourn:
Love and my nature urge me each in turn
To feed on songs that have a woeful thread.

Your words deceive. If you had any care
For those whose grief is heavy, hard to bear,
I'd waken pity out of empathy.

Singing my songs, your eyes are full of guile:
You weep with cunning like the Crocodile
To rob me of my life through trickery.[8]

---

8. The translation is mainly iambic pentameter, but with several lines in anapestic tetrameter.

Line 2: Ronsard's adjective "doucereux" can mean "full of sweetness," but also "sugary." Shakespeare's sonnets were sometimes referred to as "sugared" or "honeyed," in the sense of being mellifluous; in the dramatic context of this sonnet, however, "doucereux" seems to have negative connotations for Hélène.

11: I have translated Ronsard's word "sympathie" as "empathy," despite the fact that the latter is not part of the Renaissance lexicon, because to our ears "sympathy" is too close in meaning to "pity" to avoid what would be a tautology.

XXXVI

Vous me distes, Maistresse, estant à la fenestre,
Regardant vers Mont-martre et les champs d'alentour:
La solitaire vie, et le desert sejour
Valent mieux que la Cour, je voudrois bien y estre.

À l'heure mon esprit de mes sens seroit maistre,
En jeusne et oraison je passerois le jour,
Je desfirois les traicts et les flames d'Amour:
Ce cruel de mon sang ne pourroit se repaistre.

Quand je vous respondy, Vous trompez de penser
Qu'un feu ne soit pas feu pour se couvrir de cendre:
Sur les cloistres sacrez la flame on voit passer:

Amour dans les deserts comme aux villes s'engendre.
Contre un Dieu si puissant, qui les Dieux peut forcer,
Jeusnes ny oraisons ne se peuvent defendre.

XXXVI

You stood at the window and said to me, dear,
Looking past Montmartre's neighborhood,
That life in the desert, in solitude,
Holds more than the Court does: I'd like to be there.

I'd pass the whole day in fasting and prayer,
My spirit would master my senses; nor would
This cruel one be able to feast on my blood:
Love's arrows and flames would cause me no fear.

I answered: You think that a fire has no heat
And isn't still fire when ash covers it?
Even in cloisters one still sees Love's flame.

Love in the deserts and towns is the same:
Against such a Deity's force everlasting
There is no defense in prayers and fasting.[9]

---

9. The translation is largely in anapestic tetrameter.

Line 2: In the original French, the line literally means: "Looking toward Montmartre and the surrounding fields." Montmartre in the sixteenth century was outside the city limits of Paris.

3: Ronsard's word "desert" here and then in line 12 means a deserted, solitary place, such as the "desert fathers" might have inhabited, not necessarily our modern sense of Arabian sands.

13: In the original, Ronsard conveys the idea that the god Love is so powerful that he is able to exert his power over all the other gods.

XXXVIII

D'autre torche mon cœur ne pouvoit s'allumer
Sinon de tes beaux yeux, où l'amour me convie:
J'avois desja passé le meilleur de ma vie,
Tout franc de passion, fuyant le nom d'aimer.

Je soulois maintenant ceste dame estimer,
Et maintenant ceste autre où me portoit l'envie,
Sans rendre ma franchise à quelqu'une asservie:
Rusé je ne voulois dans les rets m'enfermer.

Maintenant je suis pris, et si je prens à gloire
D'avoir perdu le camp, frustré de la victoire:
Ton œil vaut un combat de dix ans d'Ilion.

Amour comme estant Dieu n'aime pas les superbes:
Sois douce à qui te prie, imitant le Lion.
La foudre abat les monts, non les petites herbes.

XXXVIII

No other torch could set my heart aflame
Than your bright eyes, where, drawn by Love, I came:
I'd passed the better portion of my life
Fleeing Love's name, exempt from passion's strife.

I flirted, but I never followed through,
With this or that one when I wanted to.
I always found a way that I could get
Free before I fell into the net.

But now I'm caught; and if I count it glory,
Deprived of victory, to cede territory,
Your eye is worth a ten year's Trojan War.

Love, being a God, dislikes the proud; therefore,
Be, like the lion, kind to him who pleads:
Lightning strikes mountains, not the trivial reeds.

XLIV

Comme une belle fleur assise entre les fleurs,
Mainte herbe vous cueillez en la saison plus tendre.
Pour me les envoyer, et pour soigneuse apprendre
Leurs noms et qualitez, especes et valeurs.

Estoit-ce point afin de guarir mes douleurs,
Ou de faire ma playe amoureuse reprendre?
Ou bien s'il vous plaisoit par charmes entreprendre
D'ensorceler mon mal, mes flames et mes pleurs?

Certes je croy que non: nulle herbe n'est maistresse
Contre le coup d'Amour envieilly par le temps.
C'estoit pour m'enseigner qu'il faut dés la jeunesse,

Comme d'un usufruit, prendre son passetemps:
Que pas à pas nous suit l'importune vieillesse,
Et qu'Amour et ces fleurs ne durent qu'un Printemps.

XLIV

Seated among the flowers, yourself a flower,
You gather plants, the gentlest season's dower,
To send me, and with studious care you learn
The names and qualities of each in turn.

Is this in point of fact to ease my woe
Or to reopen wounds of long ago?
Or do you want to cast a spell on me
And charm away my tears of misery?

There is no remedy, when years have passed,
For one who has been struck down by Love's strong blast.
This teaches me that from our youth we must

Enjoy life as its tenant while we may.
Importunate age pursues us day by day:
Love and the flowers have just one spring to stay.[10]

---

10. Line 12: Ronsard's line employs the legal idea of the usufruct ("usufruit"): "the right to utilize and enjoy the profits and advantages of something belonging to another."

12-14: This is one of many expressions of the *Carpe diem* ("Seize the day") theme in Ronsard's poetry.

L

Bien que l'esprit humain s'enfle par la doctrine
De Platon, qui le vante influxion des cieux,
Si est-ce sans le corps qu'il seroit ocieux,
Et auroit beau louer sa celeste origine.

Par les Sens l'ame voit, ell' oyt, ell' imagine,
Ell' a ses actions du corps officieux:
L'esprit incorporé devient ingenieux,
La matiere le rend plus parfait et plus digne.

Or' vous aimez l'esprit, et sans discretion
Vous dites que des corps les amours sont pollues.
Tel dire n'est sinon qu'imagination

Qui embrasse le faux pour les choses cognues:
Et c'est renouveller la fable d'Ixion,
Qui se paissoit de vent et n'aimoit que des nues.

L

Though the human spirit is inflated by
Plato, who boasts it emanates from on high,
Without the body it would praise in vain
(Being inert) its heavenly origin.

Soul, through the senses, sees, forms images,
Is active through the body's offices:
The spirit acquires genius when matter
Renders it worthier and makes it better.

You love the spirit and, ill-advisedly,
"Love is defiled by bodies," you declare.
That claim is nothing more than fantasy,

Which cleaves to falsehoods as if they were known,
Renewing the old fable of Ixion,
Who loved what was but cloud and fed on air.[11]

---

11. For Plato, the soul is immortal and independent of the body, whereas for Aristotle it is mortal and is that which gives life to the body. This is one of a number of sonnets in Ronsard's œuvre that enacts an opposition between these two philosophical tendencies.

Lines 1-2: Although "s'enfle" (blown up or inflated) is used ironically here, the word is derived from one designating "breath," just as "spirit" is. The translation makes the verb passive, but Ronsard wittily uses the active voice to combine two separate meanings. The literal meaning, "Though the human spirit inflates itself through Plato's doctrine," also has the connotation, "Though Plato's doctrine inflates the human spirit."

3: Randle Cotgrave's *Dictionarie of the French and English Tongues* (1611) defines "ocieux" as "idle" or "having little to do"; the word is no longer in currency and has been replaced by "oisif." My sense is that Ronsard's meaning is "inert"—i.e. inactive and without the capacity for action.

7: Literally: The incorporated spirit becomes ingenious. ("Ingenieux" is derived from "genie," which means "spirit" as well as "genius.")

11: The word that ends the line in the French, "imagination," has the meaning of "fantasy" in Ronsard's era.

13: On the fable of Ixion, see Sonnet XI of *The Love Poems for Cassandra* above.

LIII

J'errois à la volee et, sans respect de lois,
Ma chair dure à donter me commandoit à force,
Quand tes sages propos despouillerent l'escorce
De tant d'opinions que frivoles j'avois.

En t'oyant discourir d'une si saincte vois,
Qui donne aux voluptez une mortelle entorce,
Ta parole me fist par une douce amorce
Contempler le vray bien duquel je m'esgarois.

Tes mœurs et ta vertu, ta prudence et ta vie
Tesmoignent que l'esprit tient de la Déité:
Tes raisons de Platon, et ta Philosophie,

Que le vieil Promethee est une verité,
Et qu'apres que du Ciel eut la flame ravie
Il maria la Terre à la Divinité.

LIII

Without respect for law I wandered recklessly,
My unsubdued desires holding me in their sway,
When your sage admonitions stripped the rind away
Of all of those opinions that I'd held frivolously.

In hearing you discourse in such a saintly way,
Which gives a mortal sting to sensuality,
I took the gentle bait your speech now offered me
To contemplate the truth from which I'd gone astray.

Your habits and your virtue, prudence, whole life even,
Bear witness that the spirit cleaves to the Deity:
Your reasonings from Plato, entire philosophy,

That the old Prometheus is a verity,
And that when the fire was stolen out of Heaven
The Titan married Earth unto Divinity.[12]

---

12. The translation is in iambic hexameter.

It is difficult to discern whether Ronsard is writing straightforwardly or ironically (and perhaps facetiously) in this sonnet. The "Platonic" philosophy he embraces, as a result of the admonitions of Hélène, is certainly at odds with the main tenor of his thought, and even with #L above. Moreover, his interpretation of the Prometheus story is odd: Ronsard is generally desirous of marrying "Earth unto Divinity," but this aim is not consistent with Plato's doctrine, and the myth is usually interpreted as one in which the gods punish human beings for their *hubris*.

Line 12: The Titan Prometheus stole fire from the gods and was punished by being chained to a rock; his liver was eaten daily by an eagle, but grew back each night. The story is told by Hesiod in both the *Theogony* and the *Works and Days*.

LX

J'attachay des bouquets de cent mille couleurs,
De mes pleurs arrosez harsoir dessus ta porte:
Les larmes sont les fruicts que l'Amour nous apporte,
Les soupirs en la bouche, et au cœur les douleurs.

Les pendant je leur dy, Ne perdés point vos fleurs
Que jusques à demain que la cruelle sorte:
Quand elle passera, tombez de telle sorte
Que son chef soit mouillé de l'humeur de mes pleurs.

Je reviendray demain. Mais si la nuict, qui ronge
Mon cœur, me la donnoit par songe entre mes bras,
Embrassant pour le vray l'idole du mensonge,

Soulé d'un faux plaisir je ne reviendrois pas.
Voyez combien ma vie est pleine de trespas,
Quand tout mon reconfort ne depend que du songe!

LX

I fastened bouquets of flowers of many colors
Over your door last night, soaked with my tears:
Tears are the fruits the love-god Amor bears,
With sighs for our mouths and grief for these hearts of ours.

Don't shed your flowers until the morning hours
(I said as I hung them) when the cruel one fares
Forth; then, as she passes by you unawares,
Fall, so my tears rain down with the flowers.

I'll come back tomorrow. But if heart-gnawing night
Placed her in my arms in a dream of delight,
Embracing what doesn't exist, merely seems,

And soothed by false pleasure, I'd come back no more.
You see how death darkens my life at its core,
When what gives me comfort depends on mere dreams.[13]

---

13. Line 11: Ronsard's phrase is "l'idole du mensonge"—"the idol of a lie." This sonnet may be compared with #CXCII of the Cassandra poems where in line 3 of the French Ronsard uses the phrase "idole gaillarde" ("lusty idol").

Le Second Livre des Sonnets pour Hélène

I

Soit qu'un sage amoureux ou soit qu'un sot me lise,
Il ne doit s'esbahir voyant mon chef grison,
Si je chante d'amour: tousjours un vieil tison
Cache un germe de feu sous une cendre grise.

Le bois verd à grand peine en le soufflant s'attise,
Le sec sans le souffler brusle en toute saison.
La Lune se gaigna d'une blanche toison,
Et son vieillard Tithon l'Aurore ne mesprise.

Lecteur, je ne veux estre escolier de Platon,
Qui la vertue nous presche, et ne fait pas de mesme:
N'y volontaire Icare ou lourdaut Phaëthon,

Perdus pour attenter une sotise extrême:
Mais sans me contrefaire ou Voleur ou Charton,
De mon gré je me noye et me brusle moy-mesme.

From *The Second Book Of Sonnets For Hélène*

I

Whether a foolish or wise lover read,
He shouldn't marvel, seeing my graying head,
If I should sing of love: beneath gray cinders
A germ of fire smolders in its embers.

And while it's hard to get the green wood going,
A dry log blazes without any blowing.
A white fleece gained the Moon, and her old man,
Tithonus, was not disdained by Dawn.

I do not want to be the acolyte
Of Plato, preaching virtue but insincere,
Or like a willful Icarus taking flight,

Or foolish Phaethon: the Flier and Charioteer
I do not emulate, but all the same
I'm drowning myself and scorching myself with flame.[1]

---

1. Lines 7-8: Pan was able to seduce the Moon goddess Selene by covering himself in white fleeces. The fleece ("toison") is here a metaphor for white hair. Tithonus was a mortal youth beloved by Eos (Aurora), the goddess of the dawn. She asked Zeus to make him immortal, but neglected to ask that he be granted eternal youth.

11: On Icarus, see Sonnet CLXXIII of *The Love Poems for Cassandra*.

12: When Phaethon drove the chariot of the sun god Helios too close to the sun, he was struck down by Zeus and fell into the sea.

XXVI

Au milieu de la guerre, en un siecle sans foy,
Entre mille procez, est-ce pas grand' folie
D'escrire de l'Amour? De manotes on lie
Les fols qui ne sont pas si furieux que moy.

Grison et maladif r'entrer dessous la loy
D'Amour, ô quelle erreur! Dieux, merci je vous crie.
Tu ne m'es plus Amour, tu m'es une Furie,
Qui me rens fol enfant et sans yeux comme toy:

Voir perdre mon païs, proye des adversaires,
Voir en nos estendars les fleurs de lis contraires,
Voir une Thébaïde et faire l'amoureux!

Je m'en vais au Palais: adieu vieilles Sorcieres!
Muses je prens mon sac, je seray plus heureux
En gaignant mes procez, qu'en suivant vos rivieres.

XXVI

In the midst of the war, in an age without faith,
And hounded by lawsuits almost to death,
To be writing of love—is this not lunacy?
They put chains on madmen less crazy than me.

To be subject once more, although ailing and gray,
To Love—what an error! Gods, help me, I pray.
You are no longer Love but a Fury I rue.
You have blinded me, made me an infant like you.

To see my lost country the enemy's prey,
On our standards our lilies opposed in the fray:
To see a Thebaid and be playing with dreams.

I'm going to the law-courts—old Witches, adieu—
With my satchel of documents, Muses: I'm through!
I'll be happier winning than following your streams.[2]

---

2. The translation is in anapestic tetrameter.

Lines 1-2: In all likelihood, this sonnet was written around 1571, during the civil wars in France between the Catholic and Protestant forces, and at a time when a three-year lawsuit in which Ronsard was involved came to a conclusion (see the Pléiade edition, 1.1386-87).

5-6: The enjambment in the French ("dessous la loy / D'Amour") involves a witty pun because the sonnet deals both with love and with a law suit.

7: The Furies (*Erinyes*) in Greek mythology were ancient female figures who dragged murderers and other malefactors to their punishment.

10: The lily is the symbol of France; apparently, both of the combatant armies exhibited it on their standards.

11: The *Thebaid* is an epic poem of twelve books in Latin hexameters by the poet Statius (45-96 C.E.) that deals with the civil war in Thebes. In the French idiom, "to see a Thebaid" is to see a deserted place.

12-13: The Witches of line 12 ("Sorcieres" in the French) are the Muses, to whom Ronsard then explicitly refers in line 13.

XLI

Laisse de Pharaon la terre Egyptienne,
Terre de servitude, et vien sur le Jourdain:
Laisse moy ceste Court et tout ce fard mondain,
Ta Circe, ta Sirene, et ta magicienne.

Demeure en ta maison pour vivre toute tienne,
Contente toy de peu: l'âge s'enfuit soudain.
Pour trouver ton repos, n'atten point à demain:
N'atten point que l'hyver sur les cheveux te vienne.

Tu ne vois à ta Cour que feintes et soupçons:
Tu vois tourner une heure en cent mille façons:
Tu vois la vertu fausse, et vraye la malice.

Laisse ces honneurs pleins d'un soing ambitieux,
Tu ne verras aux champs que Nymphes et que Dieux,
Je seray ton Orphee, et toy mon Eurydice.

XLI

Leave the Egyptian land behind—from Pharaoh's land go free.
Come to the Jordan: leave behind this land of slavery.
I beg you leave this Court with all its worldly trumpery,
Your Circe and your Siren, and all of your sorcery.

Dwell tranquilly in your own home—none but yourself obey.
Content yourself with little: time is swift and hastes away.
To find repose, don't put things off until another day—
Until the winter snows upon your head have come to stay.

There's nothing to be found at Court but feigning and suspicion.
At every hour of the day, things twist and change position.
All virtue is corrupted there by malice and ambition.

Forget the honors for which you strove with so much urgency.
Go forth into the fields—the Nymphs and Gods are there to see.
I will be your Orpheus, and you my Eurydice.[3]

---

3. The translation is in "fourteeners"—iambic heptameter with the caesura usually falling after the fourth foot.

Lines 1-2: The "Egyptian land" is an old metaphor for slavery; the Jordan River, by contrast, is where the Israelites passed into the Promised Land.

4: Circe is the sorceress in the *Odyssey* who turned Odysseus's men into swine. The Sirens, also in the *Odyssey*, were female figures who bewitched and shipwrecked sailors by means of their beautiful songs.

11: Literally: "You see false virtue and true malice [there]."

14: Orpheus is the archetypal poet, whose songs enchanted the trees and rocks. His wife, Eurydice, descended to Hades after being bitten by a snake. Orpheus was allowed to bring her back to the upper world (to life) on condition that he not look back at her; but when he was unable to resist glancing at her, she was lost to him forever.

XLII

Ces longues nuicts d'hyver, où la Lune ocieuse,
Tourne si lentement son char tout à l'entour,
Où le Coq si tardif nous annonce le jour,
Où la nuict semble un an à l'ame soucieuse:

Je fusse mort d'ennuy sans ta forme douteuse,
Qui vient par une feinte alleger mon amour,
Et faisant toute nue entre mes bras sejour,
Me pipe doucement d'une joye menteuse.

Vraye tu es farouche, et fiere en cruauté:
De toy fausse on jouyst en toute privauté.
Pres ton mort je m'endors, pres de luy je repose:

Rien ne m'est refusé. Le bon sommeil ainsi
Abuse par le faux mon amoureux souci.
S'abuser en amour n'est pas mauvaise chose.

XLII

Those long winter nights when the sluggish Moon bears
In her slow-moving circuit her car on its way,
When the Rooster so tardily trumpets the day,
And the night seems a year to a soul full of cares:

I would die of anguish if your form, which appears
As a wavering phantom, didn't come to allay
My longing, and, naked, in my arms didn't stay,
Taking me with a false joy unawares.

The real you is proud and fierce in its cruelty;
The false one's enjoyed in total privacy.
I sleep with your specter and unto it cling.

Nothing's refused me: the good sleep I know
Deludes, through the false one, my amorous woe.
Self-delusion in love is no bad thing.[4]

---

4. The translation is mainly anapestic tetrameter.

Line 5: As the editors of the Pléiade edition note (1.1390), Ronsard is here thinking of the Greek concept of the *eidolon* (apparition or ghost), which can be a phantom of either a living or a dead person. Homer and Euripides invoke the *eidolon* of Helen of Troy, and here Ronsard is extending the idea to Hélène de Surgères.

XLIII

Quand vous serez bien vieille, au soir à la chandelle,
Assise aupres du feu, devidant et filant,
Direz chantant mes vers, en vous esmerveillant,
Ronsard me celebroit du temps que j'estois belle.

Lors vous n'aurez servante oyant telle nouvelle,
Desja sous le labeur à demy sommeillant,
Qui au bruit de mon nom ne s'aille resveillant,
Benissant vostre nom de louange immortelle.

Je seray sous la terre et fantôme sans os
Par les ombres myrteux je prendray mon repos:
Vous serez au fouyer une vieille accroupie,

Regrettant mon amour et vostre fier desdain.
Vivez, si m'en croyez, n'attendez à demain:
Cueillez dés aujourdhuy les roses de la vie.

XLIII

Some evening when you're old—the light begins to wane;
You're spinning thread beside the fire and winding off the skein;
Suddenly you recall the lines I spun and sung:
"I was the inspiration for Ronsard when I was young."

You'll be without a servant who hears what you have said,
And, drowsy from her labor, only yearns to be in bed,
But at the sound of Ronsard, risen, will not raise
Blessings upon your very name with immortal praise.

I'll be beneath the earth, a phantom without bones,
A shade who's gone to take his rest where myrtles cast their shade;
You'll be at the hearth, like other withered crones,

Thinking upon my love and on your proud disdain with sorrow.
If you believe me, live! Don't wait until tomorrow:
Gather the roses life holds out before they start to fade.[5]

---

5. The translation is in "Poulter's Measure"—alternating lines of iambic hexameter and iambic heptameter. For a discussion of this poem, see the Introduction.

Line 2: The trope of the woman weaving goes back to Homer, where it is frequently a metaphor for the poetic process—especially in the case of Helen in the *Iliad*, who is weaving the story of the Trojan War.

10: The repetition of "shade" in the translation, with its two meanings, makes what is perhaps implicit in the French explicit.

14: This is one of the most direct expressions of the *Carpe diem* topos in Ronsard's poetry. In English poetry, the theme is often associated with Robert Herrick's poem, "To the Virgins to Make Much of Time" (1648), which begins, "Gather ye rosebuds while ye may," and which may well have been influenced by Ronsard's sonnet.

XLIX

Le soir qu'Amour vous fist en la salle descendre
Pour danser d'artifice un beau ballet d'Amour,
Vos yeux, bien qu'il fust nuict, ramenerent le jour,
Tant ils sceurent d'esclairs par la place respandre.

Le ballet fut divin, qui se souloit reprendre,
Se rompre se refaire, et tour dessus retour
Se mesler s'escarter se tourner à l'entour,
Contre-imitant le cours du fleuve Meandre:

Ores il estoit rond ores long or' estroit,
Or' en poincte en triangle en la façon qu'on voit
L'escadron de La Grue evitant la froidure.

Je faux, tu ne dansois, mais ton pied voletoit
Sur le haut de la terre: aussi ton corps s'estoit
Transformé pour ce soir en divine nature.

XLIX

That evening when Love guided you to come
Down to the hall to dance Love's own ballet,
Your eyes, though it was night, restored the day:
So many beams they flashed across the room.

The ballet was divine: it seemed to waver,
Break off, re-form, and circle time after time,
Merging and parting as if thus to mime
The winding course of the Maeander River.

Now round it was, now long, and now drawn in,
Triangle-shaped sometimes, as when is seen
A flight of Cranes from the cold season fleeing.

You didn't dance—your feet while fluttering ranged
Above the ground; your body too was changed
For that one evening to immortal being.[6]

---

6. Line 8: The Maeander River was so famous in antiquity for its many windings that its name gave rise to the verb "meander." It rises in Anatolia, Turkey (Phrygia in ancient geography) and runs to the Aegean Sea. Homer mentions it in the *Iliad* in his catalogue of Trojans.

LXV

Je ne serois marry si tu contois ma peine,
De conter tes degrez recontez tant de fois:
Tu loges au sommet du Palais de nos Rois:
Olympe n'avoit pas la cyme si hautaine.

Je pers à chaque marche et le pouls et l'haleine:
J'ay la sueur au front, j'ay l'estomac penthois,
Pour ouyr un nenny un refus une vois
De desdain de froideur et d'orgueil toute pleine.

Tu es comme Deesse assise en tres-haut lieu.
Pour monter en ton ciel je ne suis pas un Dieu.
Je feray de la court ma plainte coustumiere,

T'envoyant jusq'en haut mon cœur devotieux.
Ainsi les hommes font à Jupiter priere:
Les hommes sont en terre, et Jupiter aux cieux.

LXV

If you counted my sufferings I wouldn't complain
Of counting the steps of your staircase in vain.
You lodge where the Palace juts into the sky:
Even Olympus had no peak so high.

At each step, pulse racing, I feel I shall die,
My chest racked with gasping, sweat blinding my eye—
All this just to hear your refusal again
From a voice filled with coldness, with pride, and disdain.

You're like a great Goddess in her high abode:
To ascend to your heaven I am not a God.
I shall make my complaint from the courtyard below,

And send my devotions on high up to you.
Thus men make their prayers to Jove up above;
For men are on earth, in the heavens is Jove.[7]

---

7. The translation is mainly in anapestic tetrameter.

Lines 1-2: The original contains three (not two) repetitions of the verb "conter." In line 1, "count" means "consider" or "take account of." In line 2, the verb in its first appearance literally refers to counting, but in its second appearance it can mean either "re-counted" (i.e. "counted again") or "recounted" ("retold").

4: Olympus is the mountain on which Zeus and the Olympian gods lived.

12: Ronsard's phrasing is rather sly in that "cœur devotieux" can mean either devoted or devout heart.

LXXV

Je m'enfuy du combat, mon armee est desfaite:
J'ay perdu contre Amour la force et la raison:
Ja dix lustres passez, et ja mon poil grison
M'appellent au logis et sonnent la retraite.

Si comme je voulois ta gloire n'est parfaite,
N'en blasme point l'esprit, mais blasme la saison:
Je ne suis ny Pâris, ny desloyal Jason:
J'obeis à la loy que la Nature a faite.

Entre l'aigre et le doux, l'esperance et la peur,
Amour dedans ma forge a poly cest ouvrage.
Je ne me plains du mal, du temps ny du labeur,

Je me plains de moymesme et de ton faux courage.
Tu t'en repentiras, si tu as un bon cœur,
Mais le tard repentir n'amande le dommage.

LXXV

I flee from the battle, my troops in defeat,
For Love has deprived me of strength and of reason.
I'm five decades old—my gray hairs commit treason:
They're calling me home as they sound the retreat.

If your glorification is not yet complete,
Do not blame the spirit, blame only the season.
I am neither Paris nor disloyal Jason:
I'm obeying the law that Nature has set.

Between the hope and the fear, the sweet and the bitter,
Love polished this work in my forge. My lament
Is not for the toil nor the time that I've spent.

My lament's for myself and the falsehoods you utter.
If you are kind-hearted, you will repent.
But a tardy repentance will not make things better.[8]

---

8. The translation is in anapestic tetrameter.

Line 1: A metaphor for giving up the "struggle" to "win" Hélène. The French still have the proverbial expression "hors du combat" ("out of the battle") for this kind of withdrawal.

3: Ronsard's clause, "Ja dix lustres passez," means "Almost ten *lustra* [have] passed." A Roman *lustrum* was a period of five years; hence my "five decades." This is not necessarily precise, however, because the French "lustre" in the sixteenth century may have been somewhere between four and five years. Randle Cotgrave's *Dictionarie of the French and English Tongues* (1611) defines it as "a terme of foure yeares, or fiftie moneths." In any event, Ronsard was in his fifth decade. "Commit treason" is my interpolation; the idea, however, is that his gray hairs "betray" him (i.e. the body is weak though the spirit is willing).

7: Paris, the prince of Troy in the *Iliad*, because he "stole" Helen from King Menelaus of Sparta (although she was given to him by Aphrodite after he chose her as the most beautiful of the goddesses); Jason, the hero, because, after winning the Golden Fleece with the assistance of Medea, he abandoned her.

12: Literally: "and your false promises."

Elegie

    Six ans estoit coulez, et la septiesme annee
Estoit presques entiere en ses pas retournee,
Quand loin d'affection, de desir et d'amour,
En pure liberté je passois tout le jour,
Et franc de tout soucy qui les ames devore,
Je dormois dés le soir jusqu'au point de l'aurore.
Car seul maistre de moy j'allois plein de loisir,
Où le pied me portoit, conduit de mon desir,
Ayant tousjours és mains pour me servir de guide
Aristote ou Platon, ou le docte Euripide,
Mes bons hostes muets, qui ne faschent jamais:
Ainsi que je les prens, ainsi je les remais.
Ô douce compagnie et utile et honneste!
Un autre en caquetant m'estourdiroit la teste.
    Puis du livre ennuyé, je regardois les fleurs,
Fueilles tiges rameaux especes et couleurs,
Et l'entrecoupement de leurs formes diverses,
Peintes de cent façons, jaunes rouges et perses,
Ne me pouvant saouler, ainsi qu'en un tableau,
D'admirer la Nature, et ce qu'elle a de beau:
Et de dire en parlant aux fleurettes escloses:
«Celuy est presque Dieu qui cognoist toutes choses,
Esloigné du vulgaire, et loin des courtizans,
De fraude et de malice impudens artizans.
    Tantost j'errois seulet par les forests sauvages
Sur les bords enjonchez des peinturez rivages,

Elegy

    Six years had run, and now the seventh one,[9]
Turned back upon its steps, was almost done,
When, unaffected by love's malady,
I passed each day in perfect liberty,
And free from every soul-devouring care,
Would sleep from evening till the dawn drew near.
Sole master of myself, I was at leisure
To come and go according to my pleasure,
Guided by Aristotle, Plato, and
Learned Euripides always at hand—
Good, silent guests who never make me frown
Whether I take them up or lay them down:
Sweet company, honest and full of gain!
Others by prattling would numb my brain.[10]
    Then, tired of books, I'd turn my gaze on flowers—
Their leaves, stems, shoots, their different types and colors,
The intermingling of their forms and hues,
Painted a hundred ways—reds, yellows, blues.
Unable to get my fill of marveling,
As with a picture, at each lovely thing,
I'd say unto each tender bud and bloom,
"That man is like a god if he should come
To knowledge, keeping far from the madding crowd
Of courtiers—shameless artisans of fraud."[11]
    Sometimes I wandered through the woods alone
Over the riverbanks where moss was strewn,

---

9. This poem, published for the first time in the 1584 edition of Ronsard's poetry, is placed near the end of *The Second Book of Sonnets for Hélène*.

10. As the editors of the Pléiade edition point out (1.1400), Euripides was the author of a now lost tragedy on the figure of Helen. But Renaissance authors often placed Euripides above Aeschylus and Sophocles in importance.

11. "Far from the madding crowd" is an interpolation from Thomas Gray's *Elegy Written in a Country Churchyard* (1751). Literally: "Separated from the crowd, and far from courtiers, impudent artificers of fraud and malice."

Tantost par les rochers reculez et deserts,
Tantost par les taillis, verte maison des cerfs.
    J'aimois le cours suivy d'une longue riviere,
Et voir onde sur onde allonger sa carriere,
Et flot à l'autre flot en roulant s'attacher,
Et pendu sur le bord me plaisoit d'y pescher,
Estant plus resjouy d'une chasse muette
Troubler des escaillez la demeure secrette,
Tirer avecq' la ligne en tremblant emporté
Le credule poisson prins a l'haim apasté,
Qu'un grand Prince n'est aise ayant prins à la chasse
Un cerf qu'en haletant tout un jour il pourchasse.
Heureux, si vous eussiez d'un mutuel esmoy
Prins l'apast amoureux aussi bien comme moy,
Que tout seul j'avallay, quand par trop desireuse
Mon ame en vos yeux beut la poison amoureuse.
    Puis alors que Vesper vient embrunir nos yeux,
Attaché dans le ciel je contemple les cieux,
En qui Dieu nous escrit en notes non obscures
Les sorts et les destins de toutes creatures.
Car luy, en desdaignant (comme font les humains)
D'avoir encre et papier et plume entre les mains,
Par les astres du ciel qui sont ses characteres,
Les choses nous predit et bonnes et contraires:
Mais les hommes chargez de terre et du trespas
Mesprisent tel escrit, et ne le lisent pas.
Or le plus de mon bien pour decevoir ma peine,
C'est de boire à longs traits les eaux de la fontaine

Or amid isolated rocks did roam,
Or thickets where the deer make their green home.
   I loved to trace a river to its source
And see how wave on wave prolonged its course,
One billow to another billow joined.
I loved to fish, upon a bank inclined,
Being more delighted by the silent hunt
That troubled the scaly race's secret haunt—[12]
To pull in line and bear off all aquiver
The unsuspecting fish hooked from the river—
Than a great prince derives from having caught
The stag that all day breathlessly he sought.
I'd have been glad if you, along with me,
Had taken love's bait—but it was not to be:
Wanting so much, I swallowed it alone,
Drank from your eyes the amorous poison down.
   When the evening star brings darkness to our eyes,[13]
Fixing my gaze I contemplate the skies,
In which God charts in markings plain to see
The fates of all created things; for he,
Disdaining to make use (as humans would)
Of pen and ink, foretells things bad and good.
But though the destinies that he designs
Are written in the stars, which are his signs,
Burdened by dust and death, men do not heed them:
Scorning such writings they decline to read them.
   Now what beguiles me of my suffering[14]
Is to drink deep the waters of the spring

---

12. "Scaly race" is a translation of Ronsard's synecdoche in "Troubler des escaillez la demeure secrette"—literally: "Trouble the scaled ones [i.e. fish] in their secret home." This sort of synecdoche is a frequently used trope in the Renaissance.

13. Ronsard refers to the evening star as Vesper, its Latin name; the Greek is Hesperos.

14. There is no paragraph indent in the French original (see the *Pléiade* edition 1.421), but I am inserting one in the translation to mark a thematic transition.

Qui de vostre beau nom se brave, et en courant
Par les prez vos honneurs va tousjours murmurant,
Et la Royne se dit des eaux de la contree:
Tant vault le gentil soin d'une Muse sacree,
Qui peult vaincre la mort, et les sorts inconstans,
Sinon pour tout jamais, au moins pour un long temps.
Là couché dessus l'herbe en mes discours je pense
Que pour aimer beaucoup j'ay peu de recompense,
Et que mettre son cœur aux Dames si avant,
C'est vouloir peindre en l'onde et arrester le vent:
M'asseurant toutefois qu'alors que le vieil âge
Aura comme un sorcier changé vostre visage,
Et lors que vos cheveux deviendront argentez,
Et que vos yeux, d'amour ne seront plus hantez,
Que tousjours vous aurez, si quelque soin vous touche,
En l'esprit mes escrits, mon nom en vostre bouche.
    Maintenant que voicy l'an septiéme venir,
Ne pensez plus Helene en vos laqs me tenir.
La raison m'en delivre, et vostre rigueur dure,
Puis il fault que mon age obeysse à Nature.

That boasts your beauteous name, as through the meads,
Murmuring your virtues, it forever speeds,
And is called Queen of all our waters here.[15]
Such is a sacred Muse's kindly care
That she can vanquish death and destiny—
For a long time, if not eternally.
There on the grass I lie, and think it hard
That loving so much I've gained such scant reward:
Revealing one's heart to Ladies in the end
Is trying to paint the wave and curb the wind.
I reassure myself that when old age
Shall like a sorcerer your visage change,
And when your hair has turned a silvery white,
And love no longer makes your eyes shine bright,
If any care still touches you, you'll find
My name upon your lips, my writings in your mind.
    The seventh year, Hélène, is drawing near:
Don't think you'll always hold me in your snare.[16]
Reason and your harsh cruelty set me free,
And age obliges me: I must obey.[17]

---

15. If there is a spring or stream that bears the name of Hélène, the editors of the Pléiade have not supplied it. But note that the passage modulates to one in which Ronsard refers to his Muse.

16. Literally: "nets."

17. Literally: "And it's necessary that my age obey Nature."

Discours des Miseres de ce Temps

À la Royne Catherine de Medicis

    Ma Dame, je serois ou du plomb ou du bois,
Si moy que la Nature a fait naistre François,
Aux races à venir je ne contois la peine
Et l'extreme malheur dont nostre France est pleine.
    Je veux de siecle en siecle au monde publier
D'une plume de fer sur un papier d'acier,
Que ses propres enfans l'ont prise et dévestue,
Et jusques à la mort vilainement batue.
    Elle semble au marchand, accueilli de malheur,
Lequel au coing d'un bois rencontre le volleur,
Qui contre l'estomac luy tend la main armée,
Tant il a l'ame au corps d'avarice affamée.
    Il n'est pas seulement content de luy piller
La bourse et le cheval: il le fait despouiller,
Le bat et le tourmente, et d'une dague essaye
De luy chasser du corps l'ame par une playe:
Puis en le voyant mort se sourit de ses coups,
Et le laisse manger aux mastins et aux loups.
Si est-ce que de Dieu la juste intelligence
Court apres le meurtrier et en prend la vengence:
Et dessus une roue (apres mille travaux)
Sert aux hommes d'exemple et de proye aux corbeaux.
Mais ces nouveaux Chrestiens qui la France ont pillée,
Vollée assassinée à force despouillée
Et de cent mille coups tout l'estomac batu
(Comme si brigandage estoit une vertu)

Discourse on the Misery of These Times

To the Queen, Catherine de Medici

 Madam, I'd have to be of lead or wood,[1]
If I, whom Nature made a Frenchman, should
Fail to recount the sufferings and strife,
The miseries with which our France is rife.
 To centuries to come I shall reveal,
With iron pen and paper made of steel,
How, by the very children she had bred,
She was stripped naked, beaten, left for dead.
 She's like a merchant whose misfortune is
To meet a thief in some dark stand of trees,
Who, having a greedy soul within his body,
Strikes with the weapon he has at the ready.
 He's not content to steal his purse and horse:
He beats and tortures him without remorse,
And with a dagger, trying to end his being,
Drives soul from body through a wound, then seeing
That he is dead, laughs at his injuries
And leaves him to the dogs and wolves—then flees.
Surely God's righteous judgment will pursue
And take its vengeance on the murderer, who,
After being tortured, stretched upon a wheel,
Serves men as an example, crows a meal.
But these new Christians who have stripped France bare,[2]
Plundered, assassinated, pillaged her,
Beaten her body with full many a blow
(As if to steal were counted virtue now),

---

1. The poem, composed in 1562, in the year that is often seen as marking the beginning of the civil wars between Catholics and Protestants, addresses Catherine de Medici (or Médicis), the queen mother, who was then regent of France. As the poem given here is the second part of Ronsard's "Discours," its actual title is "Continuation du Discours des Miseres de ce temps."
2. The "new Christians" are the Calvinists.

Vivent sans chastiment, et à les ouïr dire,
C'est Dieu qui les conduit et ne s'en font que rire.
    Ils ont le cœur si haut si superbe et si fier,
Qu'ils osent au combat leur maistre desfier.
Ils se disent de Dieu les mignons: et au reste
Qu'ils sont les heritiers du Royaume celeste:
Les pauvres insensez! qui ne cognoissent pas
Que Dieu père commun des hommes d'ici-bas
Veut sauver un chacun, et qu'à ses creatures
De son grand Paradis il ouvre les clostures.
Certes beaucoup de vuide et beaucoup vains lieux
Et de sieges seroyent sans ames dans les Cieux:
Et Paradis seroit une plaine deserte,
Si pour eux seulement la porte estoit ouverte.
    Or ces braves vanteurs controuvez fils de Dieu,
En la dextre ont le glaive et en l'autre le feu,
Et comme furieux qui frappent et enragent,
Vollent les temples saints et les villes saccagent.
    Et quoy? brusler maisons, piller et brigander,
Tuer assassiner par force commander,
N'obeir plus aux Rois amasser des armées,
Appellez-vous cela Eglises reformées?
    JESUS que seulement vous confessez ici
De bouche et non de cœur ne faisoit pas ainsi:
Et saint Paul en preschant n'avoit pour toutes armes
Sinon l'humilité les jeusnes et les larmes:
Et les Peres Martyrs aux plus dures saisons
Des Tyrans ne s'armoyent sinon que d'oraisons:
Bien qu'un Ange du Ciel à leur moindre priere
En soufflant eust rué les Tyrans en arriere.
    Par force en ne sçauroit Paradis violer:
JESUS nous a monstré le chemin d'y aller.
Armez de patience il faut suivre sa voye,
Non amasser un camp, et s'enrichir de proye.

They live unpunished, and to hear them talk,
It's God that guides them—and they think it's all a joke!
    So haughty are their hearts that they make light
Of challenging their master to a fight.
They say they are God's favorites, and even
That they are the inheritors of Heaven.
These poor mad fools! They do not seem to know
That God, our common father here below,
Wants each one saved, and opens up the gates
Of Paradise to all whom he creates.[3]
Heaven would be full of empty spaces,
Devoid of souls in all its dwelling-places,
And Paradise a wasteland through and through,
If the door opened only to that crew.
    Now these brave boasters, bogus sons of the Lord,
In the left hand fire, in the right a sword,
Like lunatics who know not what they do,
Rob holy temples and sack cities too.
    What? Burning houses, plundering, and worse,
Killing and dominating by main force,
Raising up armies, not obeying Kings,
Does Church reform consist in all these things?
    JESUS, acknowledged by your mouths alone
And not your hearts, would never thus have done;
And Saint Paul, when he preached, was armed with tears,
With abstinence, humility, and prayers;
The Father Martyrs in the harshest seasons
When Tyrants reigned had only their orisons,
Though, had they wished it, angels would have blown
The Tyrants back—they'd have been overthrown.
    Heaven cannot through violence be won:
How we can get there JESUS CHRIST has shown.
With patience armed, we must pursue his way—
Not by taking spoils and making men one's prey.

---

3. This would seem to be an implicit polemic against the Calvinist doctrine of Predestination and Election.

    Voulez-vous ressembler à ces fols Albigeois
Qui planterent leur secte avecque le harnois?
Ou à ces Arriens qui par leur frenaisie
Firent perdre aux Chestiens les villes de l'Asie?
Ou à Zvingle qui fut en guerre desconfit?
Ou à ceux le Duc de Lorraine desfit?
    Vous estes Predicans en possession d'estre
Tousjours tousjours batus: nostre Roy vostre maistre
Bien tost à vostre dam le vous fera sentir,
Et lors vous sentirez que peut le repentir.
    Tandis vous exercez vos malices cruelles,
Et de l'Apocalypse estes sauterelles,
Lesquelles aussi tost que le puis fut ouvert
D'Enfer, par qui le Ciel de nues fut couvert,
Avecque la fumée en la terre sortirent,
Et des fiers scorpions la puissance vestirent.
Ell' avoyent face d'homme et portoyent de grans dents
Tout ainsi que lions affamez et mordans.
Leur maniere d'aller en marchant sur la terre
Sembloit chevaux qui courent à la guerre,

    Would you be like those Albigensian lords
Who planted their sect, like madmen, with their swords?[4]
Or those mad Arians because of whom
Asia's cities were lost to Christendom?[5]
Or Zwingli, who, in doing battle, died,[6]
Or those the Duke of Lorraine boldly defied?[7]
    You're Preachers always ripe for the disaster
Of being beaten: this our King, your master,
Will make you feel soon—to your injury—
And then you'll know what penitence can be.
    Just as you exercise your depredations,
And are like the locusts named in Revelations,[8]
They, when the pit of Hell is opened by
That which has covered up with clouds the sky,
Along with smoke, shall rise up from the ground,
And scorpions that clothe its power shall abound.
They'll have men's faces; huge fangs will they bear;
Like famished, savage lions they'll appear;
In going and walking on the earth will fare
Like armored horses galloping to war—

---

4. The Albigensians, or Cathars, were members of a dualist religious movement in southern France that was extirpated as a result of the Albigensian Crusade (1209-29). Ronsard's comment is an odd one in that the Albigensians were pacifists.

5. Arianism is an early heresy that argued that because the Son was begotten by the Father, he should be seen as subordinate and not of the same essence as the Father. Arius (256-336) came from Egypt, and in the fourth century his adherents were especially numerous in the eastern Mediterranean.

6. The reference is to the Swiss reformer Ulrich Zwingli. In 1531, Zwingli's alliance applied a food blockade against the cantons of Switzerland. The cantons responded with an attack at a moment when Zurich was poorly prepared. Zwingli was killed in battle at the age of 47.

7. In 1526 the Duke of Lorraine victoriously opposed the German peasants who had followed Thomas Munzer in the Peasants' Revolt. Catholic authors at the time were sometimes enraged by what they considered the red herring of a "war of peasants" (see the Pléiade edition, 2.1575-76).

8. Revelations 9:3. The locusts are also the eighth plague of Egypt in Exodus.

Ainsi qu'ardentement vous courez aux combas,
Et villes et chasteaux vous renversez à bas.
    Ell' avoyent de fin or les couronnes aux testes,
Ce sont vos morions reluisans par les crestes:
Ell' avoyent tout le corps de plastrons enfermez,
Les vostres sont tousjours de corselets armez:
Comme d'un scorpion meurtriere estoit leur queue,
Meurtriers vos pistolets, vos mains et vostre veue:
Perdant estoit leur maistre, et le vostre a perdu
Le sceptre que nos Rois avoyent tant defendu.
Vous ressemblez encore à ces jeunes viperes,
Qui ouvrent en naissant le ventre de leurs meres:
Ainsi en avortant vous avez fait mourir
La France vostre mere en lieu de la nourrir.
    De Beze, je te prie escoute ma parolle
Que tu estimeras d'une personne folle:
S'il te plaist toutefois de juger sainement,
Apres m'avoir ouy tu diras autrement.
    La terre qu'aujourd'huy tu remplis toute d'armes
Et de nouveaux Chrestiens desguisez en gendarmes
(Ô traistre pieté!) qui du pillage ardans
Naissent dessous ta voix tout ainsi que des dents
Du grand serpent Thebain les hommes qui muerent
Le limon en couteaux desquels s'entretuerent,
Et nez et demy-nez se firent tous perir,
Si qu'un mesme Soleil les vit naistre et mourir.
    Ce n'est pas une terre Allemande ou Gothique,

Much in the way that you to combat run
And towns and castles ardently thrust down.
   The crowns upon their heads of gold so fine
Are like your crested helms that brightly shine;
Their bodies wholly are enclosed in plates,
And yours in turn in armored corselets;
Their tail is murderous as a scorpion's is—
Murderous your pistols, hands, and basilisk gaze.[9]
You are like baby vipers who have torn
Their mother's womb in process of being born;
And being aborted, you have killed your mother—
France—whom you should have given succor rather.
   I beg you listen to my words, De Bèze:[10]
Though you'll assume they're what a madman says,
If you judge sanely, in a way that's wise,
After you've heard me you'll think otherwise.
   You've filled this land with weapons and with new
Christians, although disguised as soldiers, who
(O treacherous piety!), hot for ill-gotten gain,
Are born beneath your influence, like the men
Who, sprung from the huge Theban serpent's teeth,
Born or half-born, caused one another's death
By turning clay to swords; so one day's Sun
Witnessed the birth and perishing of each one.[11]
   This isn't a German or a Gothic land,

---

9. The basilisk in ancient accounts is a snake or serpent whose gaze is lethal. The basilisk doesn't explicitly appear in the French text, but the Pléiade edition (2.1576) suggests that Ronsard's word "veue" is an allusion to the mortal effect of the basilisk's gaze.

10. The reference is to Théodore de Bèze (or Theodore Beza, 1519-1605), one of the most prominent of the French Protestants, who became Calvin's political successor after the latter's death in Geneva. Ronsard was well acquainted with de Bèze, who in fact was a poet as well as a theologian: in 1548 he published a collection of Latin poetry, *Juvenilia*.

11. These lines relate to the story of Cadmus, the legendary founder of Thebes, who killed a serpent that had been guarding the Castalian Spring and was ordered by Athena to sow the soil with the serpent's teeth. Armed men sprang up, and when Cadmus, urged by Athena, threw a stone into their midst, they fought and killed one another.

Ny une region Tartare ny Scythique:
C'est celle où tu nasquis, qui douce te receut,
Alors qu'à Vezelay ta mere te conceut:
Celle qui t'a nourry, et qui t'a fait apprendre
La science et les arts dés ta jeunesse tendre,
Pour luy faire service et pour en bien user,
Et non, comme tu fais, à fin d'en abuser.
  Si tu es envers elle enfant de bon courage,
Ores que tu le peux, rens-luy son nourrissage,
Retire tes soldars, et au Lac Genevois
(Comme chose execrable) enfonce leurs harnois.
  Ne presche plus en France une Evangile armée,
Un CHRIST empistollé tout noirci de fumée,
Qui comme un Mehemet va portant en la main
Un large coutelas rouge de sang humain.
Cela desplaist à Dieu, cela desplaist au Prince:
Cela n'est qu'un appast qui tire la province
À la sedition, laquelle dessous toy
Pour avoir liberté, ne voudra plus de Roy.
  Certes il vaudroit mieux à Lozanne relire
Du grand fils de Thetis les prouesses et l'ire
Faire combattre Ajax, faire parler Nestor,
Ou re-blesser Venus, ou re-tuer Hector,
Que reprendre l'Eglise, ou pour estre dit sage
Raccoustrer en sainct Paul je ne sçay quel passage.
De Beze, ou je me trompe, ou cela ne vaut pas
Que France en ta faveur face tant de combas,

Tartar or Scythian, you should understand:
This is where you were born and gently received,
And where—in Vézelay—you were conceived:
The land that nourished you and taught you both
The arts and sciences from tender youth
In order to comport yourself with honor—
Not, as you now do, hurl abuses on her.
    If you're a grateful child to her, good-hearted,
Repay her for the nurturing she imparted:
Withdraw your soldiers and—for heaven's sake—
Sink their weapons in Geneva's lake.[12]
    No longer preach an armed Evangelist,
Much less a pistol-armed smoke-blackened CHRIST,
Who, like a Mahomet, brandishes in hand
A cutlass that with human blood is stained.
To neither God nor King can this be pleasing.
It is a lure that makes men think of seizing
Power, and through your influence break free,
Rejecting Kings to have their liberty.
    It would be better to reread the entire
Story of the son of Thetis' ire
At Lausanne, fight with Ajax, talk with Nestor,
Or re-wound Venus or else re-kill Hector,[13]
Than blame the Church or—to be known as clever—
Emend Saint Paul in any text whatever.[14]
All this is not worth making France prolong
Her quarrels for your sake—unless I'm wrong—

---

12. "For heaven's sake" is my interpolation.

13. De Bèze was professor of Greek at the academy of Lausanne. The son of Thetis is Achilles; Ajax (the greater) is a warrior of great stature; Nestor is noted for his wisdom and good advice; Venus (Aphrodite) is wounded by Diomedes when she tries to protect her son, the Trojan Aeneas, from him; Hector, the leader of the Trojans, is finally killed by Achilles. All these figures and episodes are drawn from the *Iliad*.

14. Ronsard is most likely referring to de Bèze's editions and translations of the New Testament.

Ny qu'un Prince Royal pour ta cause s'empesche!
    Un jour en te voyant aller faire ton presche,
Ayant dessous un reistre une espée au costé:
Mon Dieu, ce dy-je lors, quelle sainte bonté!
Ô parolle de Dieu d'un faux masque trompée,
Puis que les Predicans preschent à coups d'espée!
Bien tost avec le fer nous serons consumez,
Puis qu'on voit de couteaux les Ministres armez.
    Et lors deux Surveillans qui parler m'entendirent,
Avec un haussebec ainsi me respondirent:
    Quoy? parles-tu de luy? qui seul est envoyé
Du Ciel pour r'enseigner le peuple desvoyé?
Ou tu es un Athée, ou quelque benefice
Te fait ainsi vomir ta rage et ta malice,
Puis que si arrogant tu ne fais point d'honneur
À ce Prophete sainct envoyé du Seigneur!
    Adonc je respondi, Appellez-vous Athée
Celuy qui dés enfance en son cœur a gardée
La foy de ces ayeuls? qui ne trouble les lois
De son païs natal les peuples ny les Rois?
Appellez-vous Athée un homme qui mesprise
Vos songes contrefaits les monstres de l'Eglise?
Qui croit en un seul Dieu, qui croit au sainct Esprit,
Qui croit de tout son cœur au Sauveur JESUS-CHRIST?
Appellez-vous Athée un homme qui deteste
Et vous et vos erreurs comme infernale peste?
Et vos beaux Predicans, qui subtils oiseleurs
Pipent le simple peuple, ainsi que basteleurs,
Lesquels enfarinez au milieu d'une place
Vont jouant finement leurs tours de passe-passe:

Discourse on the Misery of These Times

Nor that a Royal Prince should be impeached.[15]
    One day, encountering you before you preached,
I saw you had beneath your coat a sword.
What blessed sanctity, I said, Good Lord!
O word of God by falsehood's mask conveyed,
When Preachers preach with thrusts of a good sword blade,
Iron will soon consume us, end our lives,
Now that our Ministers are armed with knives.[16]
    And then two Elders, who were overhearing,
Responded to me in this manner, sneering:
    What? Do you speak of him whom Heaven has made
The only guide to a people that has strayed?
You're either an Atheist or some benefice
Has made you vomit out your rage and malice,
Since being so arrogant you don't accord
Due honor to this Prophet of the Lord!
    I answered: Do you call Atheist someone who
Since childhood in his heart has cleaved unto
The faith of his fathers and who doesn't trouble
His country's laws nor yet its kings or people?
Do you call Atheist someone who despises
Your nightmare of the Church in all its monstrous guises,
Believes in one sole God and the Holy Ghost,
With all his heart in the Savior JESUS-CHRIST?
Do you call Atheist one who hates you as well
As your vile errors as a plague of hell,
And your fine Preachers who, like cunning birders,
Fool simple people as do conjurors
With whitened faces who do sleight-of-hand
Tricks in a town's central square—to the end

---

15. The reference is to Henry of Navarre, the future King Henri IV, who vacillated between Protestantism and Catholicism. "Impeached" has its root meaning of "prevented" here: i.e., Henri, as a Protestant, was prevented from assuming the throne. The literal meaning of the line in the French is: "Nor that a royal prince should prevent himself [from assuming the throne] by taking your cause."

16. There is a subtle allusion here, from Hesiod's *Works and Days* and Ovid's *Metamorphoses*, to the Iron Age, which, like all previous ages, Zeus will bring to an end.

Et à fin qu'on ne voye en plein jour leur abus,
Soufflent dedans les yeux leur poudre d'oribus?

    Vostre poudre est crier bien haut contre le Pape,
Deschiffrant maintenant sa tiare et sa chape,
Maintenant ses pardons ses bulles et son bien,
Et plus haut vous criez estes gens de bien.

    Vous ressemblez à ceux que les fiévres insensent,
Qui cuident estre vrais tous les songes qu'ils pensent:
Toutefois la pluspart de vos Rhetoriqueurs
Vous preschent autrement qu'ils n'ont dedans les cœurs.
L'un monte sur la chaire ayant l'ame surprise
D'arrogance et d'orgueil, l'autre de convoitise,
Et l'autre qui n'a rien voudroit bien en avoir:
L'autre brusle d'ardeur de monter en pouvoir,
L'autre a l'esprit aigue qui par meinte traverse
Sous ombre des abus la verité renverse.

    Vous ne ressemblez pas à nos premiers Docteurs,
Qui sans craindre la mort ny les persecuteurs,
De leur bon gré s'offroyent eux-mesmes aux supplices,
Sans envoyer pour eux je ne sçay quels novices!

    Que vit tant à Genéve un Calvin desja vieux,
Qu'il ne se fait en France un martyr glorieux,
Souffrant pour sa parolle? ô âmes peu hardies!
Vous ressemblez à ceux qui font les Tragedies,
Lesquels sans les jouer demeurent tout craintifs,
Et en donnent la charge aux nouveaux apprentifs,
Pour n'estre point mocquez ny sifflez, si l'issue
Ne reussit à gré du peuple bien receue.

    Le peuple qui vous suit est tout empoisonné:
Il a tant le cerveau de sectes estonné,
Que toute la Rheubarbe et toute l'Anticyre
Ne luy sçauroyent guarir sa verve qui empire:
Car tant s'en faut, helas! qu'on la puisse guarir,
Que son mal le contente, et luy plaist d'en mourir.

That no one in plain day sees through their lies
When they blow patent powders into men's eyes?
  Your powder consists in clamoring against the Pope,
Deciphering his tiara and his cope;
His pardons, bulls, and riches you assail—
You're deemed the worthier the more you rail.
  You seem like those maddened by fever who
Imagine that their wildest dreams are true:
Most of your Preachers nonetheless impart
Something they do not hold within the heart.
One climbs the pulpit filled with thoughts of pleasure,
Another arrogant beyond all measure;
One who has little yearns to increase his store,
And one burns ardently to ascend to power;
Keen-minded, one goes many a crooked mile
To hide the truth beneath the shadow of his guile.
  No likeness to the Fathers do you bear:
They faced their persecutors without fear,
And gave themselves to torture with good grace—
Without sending another in their place.
  That Calvin should live in Geneva so many a year!
Why won't he come back to France and be martyred here
In glory for his convictions? Souls that tremble!
The makers of tragic poems you resemble,
Who, without playing in them, fearing shame,
On novice actors cast the entire blame
To avoid being hissed or laughed at, if indeed
The play should fail completely to succeed.
  The sects that follow you are poisoned, crazed:
They have the brains of those who are so amazed
That all the Rhubarb out of Anticyre
Could never cure their giddiness, I fear.[17]
Their illness pleases them, and if one tried
To cure them, they'd embrace it as they died.

---

17. In his *Adagia,* a text on which Ronsard frequently draws, Erasmus notes that rhubarb, which came from the town of Anticyre, served to cure madness (see the Pléiade edition, 2.1577).

Il faut, ce dites vous, que ce peuple fidelle
Soit guidé par un Chef qui prenne sa querelle,
Ainsi que Gedeon, qui seul esleu de Dieu,
Contre les Madians mena le peuple Hebrieu.
　　　Si Gedeon avoit commis vos brigandages,
Vos meurtres vos larcins vos Gothiques pillages,
Il seroit execrable: et s'il avoit forfait
Contre le droict commun il auroit tres-mal fait.
　　　De vostre election faites nous voir la Bulle,
Et nous monstrez de Dieu le sing et la cedulle:
Si vous ne la monstrez, il faut que vous croyez
Que je ne croiray pas que soyez envoyez.
　　　Ce n'est plus aujourd'huy qu'on croit en tels oracles:
Faites à tout le moins quelques petits miracles
Comme les Peres saincts qui jadis guerissoient
Ceux qui de maladie aux chemins languissoient,
Et desquels seulement l'ombre estoit salutaire.
　　　Il n'est plus question, ce dites vous, d'en faire,
La foy est approuvée: Allez aux regions
Qui n'ont ouy parler de nos religions,
Au Perou, Canada, Callicuth, Canibales,
Là monstrez par effect vos vertus Calvinales.
　　　Si tost que ceste gent grossiere vous verra
Faire un petit miracle, en vous elle croira
Et changera sa vie où toute erreur abonde:
Ainsi vous sauverez la plus grand part du monde.
　　　Les Apostres jadis preschoient tous d'un accord:
Entre vous aujourd'huy ne regne que discord:
Les uns sont Zvingliens les autres Lutheristes,
Les autres Puritains Quintins Anabaptistes,
Les autres de Calvin vont adorant les pas,
L'un est predestiné et l'autre ne l'est pas,
Et l'autre enrage apres l'erreur Muncerienne,

This faithful people must be led, you say,
By someone who will guide them in the fray,
As did the Lord's elected, Gideon,
Who led the Hebrews against Midian.[18]

If Gideon himself had done the things—
The murders, larcenies, Gothic pillagings—
That you've done, he'd be hated; had he gone
Against the common good, we'd say he'd badly done.

Of your election, let us see the Bull!
Show us that it's from God, his seal and scroll:
If you don't show it, you will have to know
That I won't know if it was sent or no.

Today we don't believe in oracles:
At least perform some few small miracles
Like those the sainted Fathers formerly
Did when they cured those with a malady;
And for them, only the shadow was salutary.

You say that it's no longer necessary:
The faith has been approved. Go to the regions
That have heard nothing said of our religions—
Peru, Canada, Calcutta, the Cannibalists:
Show them the virtues of your Calvinists.

As soon as these rude nations see you do
A minor miracle, they'll believe in you
And change their lives, where error holds full sway:
You'll save the large part of the world that way.

The Apostles formerly were in accord:
Among you now reigns nothing but discord:
Some are Zwinglians and others Lutherists,
Others Puritans, Quintins,[19] Anabaptists,
Still others pray in the way that Calvin taught,
One is predestined and the other is not,
One follows Munzer's error like a fool,[20]

---

18. See the story in the Book of Judges, chapters 6-8.

19. Quintin of Hainault was a figure in Calvin's circle whose views attracted some adherents.

20. Thomas Munzer (or Müntzer) was the leader of the German Peasants' Revolt of 1525. Captured after the Battle of Frankenhausen, he was tortured and executed.

Et bien tost s'ouvrira l'escole Bezienne.
  Si bien que ce Luther lequel estoit premier,
Chassé par les nouveaux est presque le dernier,
Et sa secte qui fut de tant d'hommes garnie,
Est la moindre de neuf qui sont en Germanie.
  Vous devriez pour le moins pour nous faire trembler,
Estre ensemble d'accord sans vous desassembler:
Car Christ n'est pas un Dieu de noise ny discorde:
Christ n'est que charité, qu'amour et que concorde,
Et monstrez clairement par la division
Que Dieu n'est point autheur de vostre opinion.
  Mais monstrez-moy quelqu'un qui ait changé de vie,
Apres avoir suivi vostre belle folie:
J'en voy qui ont changé de couleur et de teint
Hideux en barbe longue et en visage feint,
Qui sont plus que devant tristes, mornes et palles,
Comme Oreste agité des fureurs infernales.
  Mais je n'en ay point veu qui soient d'audacieux,
Plus humbles devenus plus doux ny gracieux,
De paillards continents, de menteurs veritables,
D'effrontez vergongneux, de cruels charitables,
De larrons aumosniers, et pas un n'a changé
Le vice dont il fut auparavant chargé.
  Je cognois quelques uns de ces fols qui vous suivent,
Je sçay bien que les Turcs et les Tartares vivent
Plus modestement qu'eux, et suis tout effroyé
Que mille fois le jour leur chef n'est foudroyé.
  J'ay peur que tout ainsi qu'Arrius fit l'entrée
Au Turc qui surmonta l'Asienne contrée,
Que par vostre moyen il ne se vueille armer,
Et que pour nous donter il ne passe la mer,

And soon enough there'll be a Bezian school.
   Thus, Luther, who was the first, is being chased
By newcomers and almost is the last:
His sect, which once had been adorned by many,
Is smallest now of nine in Germany.
   To make us tremble, at the least your actions
Would have to lead to unity, not factions;
For Christ is not a God of squabbling discord—
Christ is all love, all charity and concord.
You clearly demonstrate by your disunion
That God is not the source of your opinion.
   But show me anyone whose life has changed
From following you (whose mind is so deranged).
I see some whose complexions have changed color:
They have long, hideous beards, a false demeanor;
More than they were, they're sad, mournful, and pale,
Like an Orestes harried by Furies from Hell.[21]
   I haven't seen any who, from being presumptuous,
Have become humble, gentle, or gracious,
From lecherous turned continent, from lying truthful,
Modest who were shameless, generous cruel,
Almsgivers who were robbers: not one has redressed,
The vice by which he previously was possessed.
   Some of your followers are known to me:
The Turks and Tartars live more modestly
Than do these madmen, so I'm filled with dread
Lest suddenly their chief might be struck dead.
   I fear that just as Arius gave way
To Turks, who conquered much of Asia,[22] they,
Seeing the course you follow, soon will be
Emboldened and to subdue us cross the sea:

---

21. Orestes was pursued by the Furies after killing his mother Clytemnestra and her lover Aegisthus to avenge the murder of his father Agamemnon. In Aeschylus's trilogy, the *Oresteia*, the Furies are eventually transformed by Athena to the Eumenides (Kindly Ones) and Orestes is spared.

22. Arius himself never wielded political power, but some scholars in the sixteenth century viewed the kind of Islam practiced by the Turks as akin to Arianism, so perhaps Ronsard is drawing on this current of opinion.

Et que vous les premiers n'en supportiez la peine,
En pensant vous venger de l'Eglise Romaine.
«Ainsi celuy qui tend le piege decevant,
«En voulant prendre autruy se prend le plus souvent.
    La tourbe qui vous suit est si vaine et si sotte,
Qu'estant affriandée aux douceurs de la lote,
J'entens affriandée à ceste liberté
Que vous preschez par tout, tient le pas arresté
Sur le bord estranger et plus n'a souvenance
De vouloir retourner au lieu de sa naissance.
    Helas! si vous aviez quelque peu de raison,
Vous cognoistriez bien tost qu'on vous tient en prison,
Pipez, ensorcelez, comme par sa malice
Circe tenoit charmez les compagnons d'Ulysse.
    Ô Seigneur tout puissant, ne mets point en oubly
D'envoyer un Mercure avecque le Moly
Vers ce noble Seigneur, à fin qu'il l'admonneste,
Et luy face rentrer la raison en la teste,
Luy décharme les sens, luy dessille les yeux,
Luy monstre clairement quels furent ses ayeux,
Grands Rois et gouverneurs des grandes Republiques,
Tant craints et redoutez pour estre Catholiques!
    Si la saine raison le regaigne une fois,
Luy qui est si gaillard, si doux et si courtois,
Il cognoistra l'estat auquel on le fait vivre:
Et comme pour de l'or on lui donne du cuivre,
Et pour un grand chemin un sentier esgaré,
Et pour un diamant un verre bigarré.

You'll be the first to leave us in the lurch—
To take your vengeance on the Roman Church.
"Thus, he who tends to a deceiving snare,
Wanting to trap another's, traps himself still more."[23]

    Your low-life followers are so dissolute
That being besotted by the lotus fruit,
By which I understand this liberty
That you preach everywhere, they willingly
Remain on foreign shores and aren't torn
With longing to return where they were born.

    Alas! If you had any trace of reason,
You soon would know that you are held in prison,
Bewitched, beguiled by malice, as by Circe's
When she held charmed the shipmates of Ulysses.

    All-powerful Lord, keep in remembrance wholly
To send a Mercury with the gift of Moly[24]
Unto this noble Lord:[25] admonish him indeed,
And bring some reason back into his head;
Uncharm his senses, open up his sight,
Bring his illustrious ancestors to light—
Great Kings and governors of great Republics,
Held in such dread and awe for being Catholics!

    If reason is restored within his mind,
He who is so gallant, courteous, kind,
Will understand the state in which we're living,
And how for gold copper instead is given,
And for a highway a narrow, straitened pass,
And for a diamond a colored glass.[26]

---

23. As the editors of the Pléiade note (2.1578), this couplet echoes biblical adages contained in Psalms 7:16 and 9:16.

24. In Book 10 of the *Odyssey*, Hermes gives the Moly, a magic herb, to Odysseus to protect him from Circe after she had transformed all of his men to swine.

25. The reference is to the Prince de Condé (1530-69), the military leader of the French Protestants, who belonged to the House of Bourbon, the royal family.

26. These lines (with their string of parallel metaphors) are obscure. My sense is that Ronsard is saying that the Protestants, instead of accepting

Hà! que je suis marry que cil qui fut mon maistre,
Depestré du filet ne se peut recognoistre!
Je n'aime son erreur, mais hayr je ne puis
Un si digne Prelat dont serviteur je suis,
Qui benin m'a servi (quand Fortune prospere
Le tenoit pres des Rois) de Seigneur et de pere.
Dieu preserve son chef de malheur et d'ennuy,
Et le bon-heur du Ciel puisse tomber sur luy.
  Achevant ces propos je me retire, et laisse
Ces Surveillans confus au milieu de la presse,
Qui disoient que Satan le cœur m'avoit couvé,
Et me grinçant les dents m'appelloient reprouvé.
  L'autre jour en pensant que ceste pauvre terre
S'en alloit (ô malheur!) la proye d'Angleterre,
Et que ses propres fils amenoient l'estranger
Qui boit les eaux du Rhin, à fin de l'outrager:
M'apparut tristement l'idole de la France,
Non telle qu'elle estoit lors que la brave lance
De Henry la gardoit, mais foible et sans confort,
Comme une pauvre femme attainte de la mort.
Son sceptre luy pendoit, et sa robbe semée
De fleurs de liz estoit en cent lieux entamée:
Son poil estoit hideux, son œil have et profond,
Et nulle majesté ne luy haussoit le front.
  En la voyant ainsi, je luy dis: Ô Princesse,
Qui presque de l'Europe as esté la maistresse,
Mere de tant de Rois, conte moy ton malheur,
Et dy moy je te pri' d'où te vient ta douleur!
  Elle adonc en tirant sa parolle contrainte,
Souspirant aigrement, me fit ainsi sa plainte.
  Une ville est assise és champs Savoysiens,
Qui par fraude a chassé ses Seigneurs anciens,
Miserable sejour de toute apostasie,

That he who was my master (now the thread
Has been unwound) knows himself not, is sad.
I do not like his error, but won't defame
So worthy a Prelate, whose servant yet I am—
Who graciously served me (when prosperous Fortune
Held him near Kings) with the Father and the Son.
God keep his head from suffering and sadness,
And may the Heavens pour down on him their gladness.

    Ending this speech, I took my leave, and let
These Elders in the crowd's midst foam and fret:
They said that Satan hatched my heart and claimed,
Gnashing their teeth, I was among the damned.

    Thinking of this poor land the other day,
How it was going to be England's prey,
And how her sons were summoning the stranger,
Who drinks of the Rhine, to ravage and outrage her:
There came to me the specter of sad France,
Not as she was when Henry's valiant lance
Protected her,[27] but weak, without a friend,
Like a poor woman whose life was at its end.
Her lily-studded gown was ripped and mangled
In many places, and her scepter dangled;
Her hair was hideous, sunken was her eye,
And on her brow remained no majesty.

    In seeing her thus, I said to her, O Princess,
You who were practically Europe's mistress,
Mother of Kings so many, please explain
The source of your unhappiness and pain.

    Then dragging out words as if upon constraint,
Bitterly sighing, she made me this complaint.

    There is a Savoyan city that expelled—
By fraud—the Lords by whom it had been held,
And in it now dwells all apostasy,

---

the traditional Church, with its inevitable failings, are engaging in a kind of utopian thinking that will wreak havoc and ultimately make things worse than they are.

27. The reference is to Henry II, who had died in 1559.

D'opiniastreté, d'orgueil et d'heresie,
Laquelle (en ce-pendant que les Rois augmentoient
Mes bornes et bien loin pour l'honneur combatoient)
Appellant les banis en sa secte damnable,
M'a fait comme tu vois chetive et miserable.
    Or mes Rois cognoissans qu'une telle cité
Leur seroit, comme elle est, une infelicité,
Deliberoient assez de la ruer par terre:
Mais contre elle jamais n'ont entrepris la guerre:
Ou soit par negligence ou soit par le destin
Entiere ils l'ont laissée, et de là vient ma fin.
    Comme ces laboureurs, dont les mains inutiles
Laissent pendre l'hyver un toufeau de chenilles,
Dans un fueille seiche au feste d'un pommier:
Si tost que le Soleil de son rayon premier
A la fueille eschauffée, et qu'elle est arrousée
Par deux ou par trois d'une tendre rosée,
Le venin qui sembloit par l'hyver consumé,
En chenilles soudain apparoist animé,
Qui tombent de la fueille, et rampent à grand' peine
D'un dos entre-cassé au milieu de la plaine:
L'une monte en un chesne et l'autre en un ormeau,
Et tousjours en mangeant se trainent au coupeau:
Puis descendent à terre, et tellement se paissent
Qu'une seule verdure en la terre ne laissent.
    Alors le laboureur voyant son champ gasté,
Lamente pour neant qu'il ne s'estoit hasté
D'estouffer de bonne heure une telle semence:
Il voit que c'est sa faute et s'en donne l'offence.
    Ainsi lors que mes Rois aux guerres s'efforçoient,
Toutes en un monceau ces chenilles croissoient:
Si qu'en moins de trois mois telle tourbe enragée
Sur moy s'est espandue, et m'a toute mangée.
    Or mes peuples mutins, arrogans et menteurs
M'ont cassé le bras droit chassant mes Senateurs:

All obduracy, pride, and heresy.[28]
During the time my Kings were seeking glory
In foreign lands to extend my territory,
It called those banished to her damnable
Sect, and this, as you see, has made me miserable.
    Now, recognizing that this town would breed
Disasters for them, as it has indeed,
My kings considered crushing it utterly;
But whether through negligence or destiny,
Never waged war on it, left it intact:
My ruin has resulted from this fact.
    Compare those lazy laborers who leave
Caterpillars when cold days arrive
Clinging to dry leaves in the apple trees:
Soon as the Sun with its initial rays
Has warmed the leaves, and they have been anew
Two or three times moistened with gentle dew,
The tuft that winter seemed to have consumed
Wakens to caterpillars disentombed:
They fall from leaves and with arched backs they slowly
Crawl through the land till they inhabit it wholly:
One climbs an oak, another climbs an elm,
And always feeding they soon overwhelm
The earth, till from the tree-tops to the plain,
No single trace of verdure will remain.
    The laborer then, seeing his field laid waste,
Laments (to no avail) not taking haste
In snuffing out this brood the way one ought:
He blames himself and sees he is at fault.
    Thus, while my Kings in foreign wars were vying,
These caterpillars went on multiplying,
So that in three months' time a frenzied crop
Had swarmed all over me and eaten me up.
    My people now, a lying, mutinous band,
Have thrown out my Senators, breaking my right hand:[29]

---

28. Geneva, which was established as Calvinist in 1541.

29. The reference is to the members of the *parlements* perhaps expelled from towns controlled by the reformists (see the Pléiade edition, 2.1578).

Car de peur que ma loy ne corrigeast leur vice,
De mes Palais royaux ont bany la Justice:
Ils ont rompu ma robbe en rompant mes citez,
Rendans mes citoyens contre moy despitez:
Ont pillé mes cheveux en pillant mes Eglises,
Mes Eglises, helas! que par force ils ont prises,
En poudre foudroyans Images et Autels,
Venerable sejour de nos saincts immortels.
Contre eux puisse tourner si malheureuse chose,
Et l'or sainct desrobé leur soit l'or de Tholose!
    Ils n'ont pas seulement, sacrileges nouveaux,
Fait de mes temples saincts, estables à cheveaux:
Mais comme tourmentez des fureurs Stygiales
Ont violé l'honneur des Ombres sepulchrales,
Afin que par tel acte inique et malheureux
Les vivans et les morts conspirassent contre eux.
Busire fut plus dous, et celuy qui promeine
Une roche aux enfers, eut l'ame plus humaine:
Bref ils m'ont delaissé en extreme langueur.
Toutefois en mon mal je n'ay perdu le cœur,
Pour avoir une Royne à propos rencontrée,
Qui douce et gracieuse envers moy s'est monstrée:
Elle par sa vertu (quand le cruel effort
De ces nouveaux mutins me trainoit à la mort)
Lamentoit ma fortune, et comme Royne sage

They fear their vices may not go unpunished,
So from my law courts Justice has been banished.
In tearing up my cities they have torn
My garments,[30] giving me up to hate and scorn:
They rifle through my hair, rifle and plunder
My Churches, alas, tearing them asunder,
And blast to rubble image, altar, portal,[31]
The hallowed sojourn of my saints immortal.
May all these evils turn on them, and may
The gold they've looted be Toulousan gold someday.[32]

    Not only have they turned my holy temples—
As a new sacrilege—to horses' stables,
They violate the honor of the buried,
As if they were by Stygian Furies harried;
So on account of this unrighteous deed
The living join against them with the dead.
Busiris was kinder;[33] he who was forced to roll
The rock in Hades had a more human soul.[34]
In brief: I am forsaken, left to languish,
But haven't yet lost heart despite my anguish,
Having a Queen who always has been kind,
To whom I can express what's in my mind.[35]
When these new rebels in their cruelty
Were dragging me to death, she solaced me,
And as a virtuous, sagacious Queen,

---

30. Literally: have torn my robe (or dress)—an allusion to the *noblesse de robe*, and hence a metonymy for the government.

31. "Portal" is my interpolation.

32. The Pléiade edition (2.1578) notes that the "gold of Toulouse" is a proverbial expression: the Romans who pillaged the treasures of the temple of Toulouse all came to a bad end. Ronsard's source is once again Erasmus's *Adagia*.

33. Busiris, a king of Egypt and an archetype of tyranny, is said to have sacrificed all visitors to his gods.

34. A reference to Sisyphus, the king of Corinth, who also killed travelers, and who was punished by Zeus for betraying one of his secrets.

35. The reference is to Catherine de Medici, the Queen Mother, to whom the poem is dedicated and addressed.

Reconfortoit mon cœur, et me donnoit courage.
  Elle abaissant pour moy sa haute Majesté,
Preposant mon salut à son authorité,
Mesmes estant malade est maintefois allée
Pour m'appointer à ceux qui m'ont ainsi volée.
  Mais Dieu qui des malings n'a pitié ny mercy
(Comme au Roy Pharaon) a leur cœur endurcy,
À fin que tout d'un coup sa main puissante et haute
Les corrige en fureur et punisse leur faute.
Puis quand je voy mon Roy, qui desja devient grand,
Qui courageusement me soustient et defend,
Je suis toute guarie, et la seule apparance
D'un Prince si bien-né me nourrist d'esperance.
  Avant qu'il soit long temps ce magnanime Roy
Dontera les destins qui s'arment contre moy,
Et ces faux devineurs qui d'une bouche ouverte
De son sceptre Royal ont predite la perte.
  Ce-pendant pren la plume et d'un stile endurcy
Contre le trait des ans engrave tout cecy,
Afin que nos nepveux puissent un jour cognoistre
Que l'homme est malheureux qui se prend à son maistre.
  Ainsi par vision la France à moy parla,
Puis tout soudainement de mes yeux s'en-vola
Comme une poudre au vent ou comme une fumée
Qui soudain dans la nue est en rien consumée.

Lamented the sad fortune that was mine.
    She, lowering for me her high Majesty,
Protects me through her own authority;
And though she's ill, has sought to have me be
Reconciled to those who have stolen from me.
    But those whose hearts (like Pharaoh's) God has hardened
Should not expect to see their malice pardoned;
For suddenly his hand omnipotent
Will bring on them his furious punishment.
And when I see my King, grown great indeed,[36]
Who valorously defends me in my need,
I'm cured; for that he merely should appear,
A leader so well-born, gives hope and cheer.
    Before too long this great-souled King shall quell
The destinies arming themselves pell mell
Against me, and those soothsayers who boast
With wagging tongues his Scepter shall be lost.[37]
    But take your pen: in hardened style bring home
All of these things unto the years to come,
So that to our descendants it's made known:
Who quarrels with his master is undone.
    Thus in my vision France had this to say.
Then suddenly from my eyes she stole away—
Like dust in wind or smoke dissolved in air,
Which vanishes in a cloud and isn't there.

---

36. The future Charles IX, who reached his majority in 1562, the year Ronsard's *Discours* was composed. It is ambiguous in the French text whether the word "grand" refers to Charles' physical or his moral stature.

37. These lines are obscure. Ronsard seems to be responding to Protestant prognosticators who were foretelling the end of Catholic hegemony in France.

Elegie

À Philippes Des-Portes, Chartrain

    Nous devons à la Mort et nous et nos ouvrages:
Nous mourons les premiers, le long reply des âges
En roulant engloustist nos œuvres à la fin:
Ainsi le veut Nature et le puissant Destin.
    Dieu seul est eternel: de l'homme elementaire
Ne reste apres la mort ny veine ny artere:
Qui pis est, il ne sent, il ne raisonne plus,
Locatif descharné d'un vieil tombeau reclus.
    C'est un extreme abus, une extreme folie
De croire que la Mort* soit cause de la vie:
Ce sont poincts opposez autant que l'Occident
S'oppose à l'Orient, l'Ourse au Midy ardent.
    L'une est sans mouvement, et l'autre nous remue,
Qui la forme de l'ame en vigueur continue,
Nous fait ouyr et voir, juger, imaginer,
Discourir du present, le futur deviner.
    Les morts ne sont heureux, d'autant que l'ame vive**

Elegy

To Philippe Desportes of Chartres

    We owe Mortality a debt: first we ourselves must die,[1]
Then as the long unwinding train of centuries pass by,
Our works and all that we have done are swallowed up as well;
For such is mighty Destiny and such is Nature's will.
    God only is eternal: of composite man remains,[2]
After his death, nothing at all—no arteries or veins;
And, which is worse, he doesn't feel and has no power of reason,
Being the fleshless tenant of an ancient tomb, his prison.
    It is a foolish error, utter madness, to believe
That Death gives rise to Life, and after dying we shall live;*
For these two are opposed to one another, just as are
The Occident and Orient, the South and the cold North Star.[3]
    The one is without movement while the other, which imparts
Form to the soul, gives movement to all of our vital parts,[4]
Allowing us to judge and to imagine, hear and see,
Talk of the present and foretell what will and will not be.
    The dead aren't happy, as in them the soul that is perforce

---

1. The poet Philippe Desportes (1546-1606), was a popular court poet. His patron, from 1574 on, was the French king, Henry III. This is the only poem that Ronsard personally annotated; it was published for the first time in the posthumous edition of his *Œuvres Complètes* in 1587 (see Pierre de Ronsard, *Selected Poems*, ed. Malcolm Quainton and Elizabeth Vinestock [New York: Penguin, 2002], 288). The "Author's Annotations" are given at the end of the poem. The translation is in "fourteeners"—iambic heptameter couplets."
2. The phrase that I have translated as "of composite man" is "de l'homme elementaire" in the French—in other words, of man composed of elements. Ronsard's conception, borrowed from the Scholastics, is that whereas God is "simple," an entity without parts, man is composed of elements that must eventually return to the earth.
3. Ronsard refers to the constellation of the Great Bear ("l'Ourse"), or Big Dipper. The North Star, Polaris (in my altered reference), is in Ursa Minor, the Little Bear or Little Dipper.
4. Ronsard's conception is ultimately derived from Aristotle's *De Anima* (*On the Soul*). For Aristotle, the soul is the life of the body.

Du mouvement principe, en eux n'est plus active.
L'heur vient de la vertue, la vertue d'action:
Le mort privé du faire est sans perfection.
    L'heur de l'ame, est de Dieu contempler la lumiere:
La contemplation de la cause premiere
Est la seule action: contemplant elle agist:
Mais au contemplement l'heur de l'homme ne gist.
    Il gist à l'œuvre seul, impossible à la cendre
De ceux que la Mort faict soubs les ombres descendre.
C'est pourquoy de Pluton les champs deshabitez
N'ont polices ny loix ny villes ny citez.
    Or l'ouvrage et l'ouvrier font un mesme voyage,
Leur chemin est la Mort. Athenes et Carthage,
Et Rome qui tenoit la hauteur des hauteurs,
Sont poudre maintenant comme leurs fondateurs.
    Pource les Grecs ont dit que, glout de faim extreme
Saturne devoroit ses propres enfans mesme.
Le general est ferme et ne fait place au temps,
Le particulier meurt presque au bout de cent ans.
    Chacun de son labeur doit en ce monde attendre
L'usufruit seulement, que present il doit prendre
Sans se paistre d'attente et d'une eternité,***
Qui n'est rien que fumée et pure vanité.
    Homere, qui servit aux neuf Muses de guide,
S'il voyait aujourd'huy son vaillant Eacide,

The principle of movement has no longer any force;**
For happiness from virtue comes and virtue comes from action:
Deprived of their activity, the dead have no perfection.
    In contemplation of God's light, soul finds its happiness:
To contemplate the primal cause is how it gains its bliss.
This is its only action, contemplation its true station;
But happiness for man does not consist in contemplation.[5]
    It lies in the work alone, which is impossible for those
That Death has thrust beneath the earth, down among the shadows.
This is why Pluto's realm,[6] which lacks living inhabitants,
Has neither towns nor cities, neither laws nor governance.
    The worker and the work he's done go on the selfsame voyage
Along the path that Death has paved. Athens as well as Carthage,
And Rome, which occupied the heights in peacetime and in war,
Are now reduced to dust just as their founding fathers are.
    This is the reason that the Greeks told that gruesome tale
Of ravenous Saturn swallowing down his children one and all.[7]
That which is of the genus will stand firm amidst the years;
After at most a century, the species disappears.
    Each person of his labor may in this World hope to know
Only the usufruct he holds in the here-and-now;[8]
Nor should he feed on expectations of an eternity***
Which isn't anything at all but smoke and vanity.
    Homer, who served the Muses nine, guiding them on their way,

---

5. The conception that Ronsard is developing in these lines is a difficult one, but only apparently contradictory. In my view, what he is saying is that if the soul were considered as separate from the body, its action and being would reside solely in contemplation; but since the human soul exists only insofar as it is joined to the body (as in Aristotle's *De Anima*), "happiness for man does not consist [solely] in contemplation."

6. Pluto, the god of the Underworld, is the Roman name for Hades.

7. Saturn is the Roman name for the Greek god Kronos (Chronos), whose name means "time." In the story told by Hesiod in the *Theogony*, Kronos, fearing that one of his children would supplant him, swallowed them as soon as they were born. Zeus tricked him, however, and caused him to vomit them up.

8. Usufruct is a legal term that entails the right to use and enjoy someone else's property for a limited time.

Ne le cognoistroit plus, ny le docte Maron
Son Phrygien Enée. Ainsi le froid giron
De la tombe assoupist tous les sens de nature,
Qui sont deus à la terre et à la pourriture.
    Nous semblons aux Toreaux, qui de coutres trenchans,
À col morne et fumeux, vont labourant les champs,
Sillonnant par rayons une germeuse plaine,
Et toutefois pour eux inutile est leur peine:
Ils ne mangent le bled qu'ils ont ensemencé,
Mais quelque vieille paille, ou du foin enroncé.
    Le belier Colonnel de sa laineuse troupe,
L'eschine de toison pour les autres se houpe:
Car le drap, bien que sien, ne l'habille pourtant:
L'homme, ingrat envers luy au dos le va portant
Sans luy en sçavoir gré. Ainsi nostre escriture
Ne nous profite rien: c'est la race future
Qui seule en jouyst toute, et qui juge à loisir
Les ouvrages d'autruy, et s'en donne plaisir,
Rendant comme il luy plaist nostre peine estimée.
    Quant à moy, j'aime mieux trente ans de renommee,
Jouyssant du Soleil, que mille ans de renom
Lors que la fosse creuse enfouyra mon nom,
Et lors que nostre forme en une autre se change.
« L'homme qui ne sent plus n'a besoin de louange.
    Il est vray que l'honneur est le plus grand de tous
Les biens exterieurs qui sont propres à nous,
Qui vivons et sentons: les morts n'en ont que faire,

Were he to see the valiant Aeacides today,[9]
He wouldn't know him; nor would Maro if he were to come
Upon his Phrygian Aeneas.[10] Thus the grave's cold womb
Dulls and numbs the natural senses, which we must repay,
For they are owed to earth and to the process of decay.

    We are like toiling Bulls that till the fields; heavy and slow,
Their mournful necks steaming with heat, they pull the keen-edged plough,
Harrowing the furrows that will fertilize the plain.
Fruitless to them, however, is their labor and their pain:
They do not eat the wheat they've sown (their straining is in vain),
Only old straw and brambly hay—the grain is kept for men.

    The Ram that is the colonel to his wooly flock of sheep
Has fleece that tufts along his spine, but isn't his to keep.
He doesn't dress himself in cloth that from his wool was sewn:
Man wears it on his back as if he'd grown it on his own,
And doesn't show him gratitude. Our writing, in like case,
Profits us not at all; for it is only a future race
That will enjoy it as a whole and judge for itself at leisure
Works that belong to another time, giving itself that pleasure
And, as it sees fit, measuring esteem for what we've done.

    As for myself, I'd rather have thirty years of renown,
Happy beneath the Sun,[11] than a millennium of fame,
During which time the hollow grave has quite consumed my name
And we have been transformed to something other than we were.
"A man who can no longer feel has need of praise no more."[12]

    It's true that of the external goods, honor is what we deem
Greatest of those proper to man: we hold it in esteem

---

9. Aeacides (the patronymic) refers to Achilles, the grandson of Aeacus. Statius throughout his epic, *The Achilleid*, refers to the hero thus.

10. Maro is Virgil's surname; Phrygia, here a metonymy for Troy, was an ancient area and nation in western Turkey, in the midst of which Troy was located.

11. As Ronsard's "Elegy" to Desportes is strongly marked by Ecclesiastes, it is fitting that his phrase "Jouyssant du Soleil" should echo the phrase "under the sun," a frequently repeated motif of the biblical text.

12. Either a proverbial statement or one that Ronsard puts in quotation marks in order to present it as having proverbial status.

Toutefois le bien faire est chose necessaire,
Qui profite aux vivans, et plaist aux heritiers.
    Les fils de leurs ayeuls racontent volontiers
Les magnanimes faicts: la louange illustrée
D'un acte vertueux ne fut jamais frustrée
De son digne loyer, soit futur ou present.
    Le Ciel ne donne à l'homme un plus riche present
Que l'ardeur des vertus, les aimer et les suivre,
Un renom excellent, bien mourir et vivre.
    Des-Portes, qu'Aristote amuse tout le jour,
Qui honores ta Dure, et les champs qu'à l'entour
Chartres voit de son mont, et panché les regarde,
Je te donne ces vers, à fin de prendre garde
De ne tuer ton corps desireux d'acquerir
Un renom journalier qui doit bien-tost mourir:
Mais happe le present d'un cœur plein d'allegresse,
Cependant que le Prince, Amour, et la jeunesse
T'en donnent le loisir, sans croire au lendemain.
Le futur est douteux, le present est certain.

While we're alive and feel: the dead don't need it—they are through!
But doing good things nonetheless is what we ought to do:
They benefit the living and are pleasing to their heirs.
   Sons willingly recount the noble deeds of ancestors,
Such acts as are magnanimous: the fame that we accord
To virtuous actions, giving them their duly-earned reward,
Is never disappointed by the future if not the present.
   Heaven does not bestow on man any more rich a present[13]
Than seeking the virtues ardently, loving and following them,
Living well and dying well, having an excellent name.
   Desportes, you who are much engrossed in Aristotle's thought,[14]
While honoring your river Eure and the fields that lie about,
Which Chartres from its hill can see, if it looks down from there,
I offer you these verses that would urge you to take care
Not to destroy your body by being anxious to acquire
A fame that's only of its day, and thus must soon expire,[15]
But clasp hold of the present with a joyous heart, while still
The Prince[16] and Love and youth, by making all this possible,
Give you the opportunity;[17] for the morrow take no thought.[18]
The present moment's certain, but the future is in doubt.

---

13. Ronsard is very fond of rhyming the same word with different meanings. Fortunately, in this case, the English is identical to the French.

14. This is ironic for a number of reasons. For one, Ronsard was himself "engrossed in Aristotle's thought," as early passages in the poem, where he draws on *De Anima*, indicate (see above, lines 9-20). For another, in the second of his "Author's Annotations," the poet contradicts one of his (Aristotelian) assertions by attributing it to Aristotle.

15. Ronsard had asserted earlier in the poem that all fame is ephemeral, but his phrasing here ("Un renom journalier") seems to focus specifically on the kind of fame that is only of the moment and will soon fade—with the implication, perhaps, that this is the kind of fame enjoyed by Desportes.

16. Though Desportes' patron was the king, Ronsard uses the word "Prince" in the Latinate sense of leader.

17. "T'en donnent le loisir" would ordinarily mean "give you the leisure for it," but I follow Quainton and Vinestock in translating "loisir" as "opportunity" here (see *Selected Poems*, 132). I think there may also be the implication here of the Renaissance emphasis on the idea of the *occasion*, as in Machiavelli's thought.

18. Ronsard's phrase, "sans croire au lendemain"—literally: "without believing [or having faith in] the morrow"—expresses an Epicurean skepticism about the afterlife while ironically echoing the Gospel of Matthew. In the English of the King James Version: "Take therefore no thought for the morrow: for the morrow shall take thought for the things of itself. Sufficient unto the day is the evil thereof" (6:34).

Annotations de l'autheur

Que la Mort soit cause de la vie. Contre les Pythagoriques, qui pensoient qu'apres la mort nos ames revenoient en autres corps, et mesmes és bestes.

**Les morts ne sont heureux.* C'est l'opinion d'Aristote qui est faulse: car les morts qui meurent en Dieu, sont heureux parfaitement.

***D'une eternité.* Contre les Poëtes qui ne promettent autre chose à eux mesmes et aux autres par leurs vers, que l'eternité.

Author's Annotations

*Against the Pythagoreans, who thought that after death our souls returned in other bodies, and even in those of beasts.

**This is the opinion of Aristotle, which is false: for the dead that die in God are perfectly happy.[19]

***Against the Poets, who promise themselves and others only the eternity that can be attained through poetry.[20]

---

19. Ronsard's note puts ironic distance between himself and Aristotle here, but the assertion he makes in the poem itself, though derived from Aristotle, is presented as his own.

20. Quainton and Vinestock translate the sentence as follows: "Against Poets who promise themselves and others, through their verse, nothing less than eternity" (*Selected Poems*, 132). This is a possible rendering of Ronsard's grammar, but it seems to me to have little to do with the assertion in the poem that is being annotated, which is that the idea of eternity per se is mere smoke and vanity. In my view, Ronsard in his note is not only taking refuge behind the mask of Christianity but in attacking the poets' notion of eternity, according to which one can hope only for a long-lasting temporal fame (a notion that has no actual relevance to the passage in the "Elegy" itself), he is testifying to his uncomfortable awareness that the Epicurean conception he is entertaining runs counter to Christianity.

Les Derniers Vers

I

Je n'ay plus que les os, un Squelette je semble,
Decharné, denervé, demusclé, depoulpé.
Que le trait de la mort sans pardon a frappé,
Je n'ose voir mes bras que de peur je ne tremble.

Apollon et son filz deux grans maistres ensemble,
Ne me sçauroient guerir, leur mestier m'a trompé,
Adieu, plaisant soleil, mon œil est estoupé,
Mon corps s'en va descendre où tout se desassemble.

Quel amy me voyant en ce point despouillé
Ne remporte au logis un œil triste et mouillé,
Me consolant au lict et me baisant la face,

En essuiant mes yeux par la mort endormis?
Adieu chers compaignons, adieu, mes chers amis,
Je m'en vay le premier vous preparer la place.

Last Verses

I

I look like a skeleton stretched on a bier
Without muscles or sinews—I'm nothing but bone,
Which the arrow of death without mercy struck down.
I can't look at my arms without trembling with fear.

Apollo and his son, great doctors without peer,
Wouldn't know how to cure me—their craft's come undone.
My eyes have grown dim: farewell, cheerful sun,
My body's going down where all things disappear.

What friend who has seen me in such a sad plight
Won't return to his lodgings with eyes wet with tears
After giving me comfort and kissing my face,

While wiping my eyes which death's sleep has shut tight?
Farewell, dear companions, yes, farewell, my dears.
I'm going on ahead to prepare you a place.[1]

---

1. Ronsard's *Derniers Vers* were first published in a "plaquette" (a small, thin book, similar to what we would call a chapbook) after his death in 1586, then subsequently at the end of the 1587 edition of the *Œuvres complètes* (see the Pléiade edition, 2:1613).

The translation of #1 varies between iambic and anapestic tetrameter.

Line 5: Apollo is the god of medicine; his son, Asclepius, a demi-god, having been born of a mortal mother, is said to have been instructed in the art of medicine by the Centaur Chiron.

II

Meschantes nuicts d'hyver, nuicts filles de Cocyte
Que la terre engendra d'Encelade les seurs,
Serpentes d'Alecton, et fureur des fureurs,
N'approchez de mon lict, ou bien tournez plus vitte.

Que fait tant le soleil au gyron d'Amphytrite?
Leve toy, je languis accablé de douleurs,
Mais ne pouvoir dormir c'est bien de mes malheurs
Le plus grand, qui ma vie chagrine et despite.

Seize heures pour le moins je meur les yeux ouvers,
Me tournant, me virant de droit et de travers,
Sus l'un, sus l'autre flanc je tempeste, je crie,

Inquiet je ne puis en un lieu me tenir,
J'appelle en vain le jour, et la mort je supplie,
Mais elle fait la sourde, et ne veut pas venir.

II

Vile winter nights, nights, daughters of Cocytus,
You earth-engendered sisters of Enceladus,
Serpents of Alecto, and Furies most furious,
Don't come near my bed with your cold winds injurious.

Why lingers the Sun in the bosom of Amphitrite?
Rise, for I languish, oppressed by my plight, the
Worst aspect of which is insomnia nightly,
Continually vexing and seeming to spite me.

At least sixteen hours, eyes open, I die,
Tossing to right and to left in my pain;
On one or the other side, raging, I cry,

Unable in any one place to lie calm.
I call vainly for day, and for death pray in vain:
She pretends to be deaf and refuses to come.[2]

---

2. The translation varies between iambic pentameter and anapestic tetrameter.

Line 1: In Greek mythology, Cocytus, the river of lamentation, is one of the five rivers of the Underworld. The inhabitants of the ninth circle of Dante's *Inferno* are frozen in its waters.

2: Gaia (the Earth) and Ouranos (the Sky) gave birth to the Giants, among whom was Enceladus. In some traditions, the Giants fought and were defeated by the Olympian gods. Ronsard seems to have invented the daughters of Cocytus and the sisters of Enceladus: I find no reference to them elsewhere.

3: Alecto is one of the Furies (or Erinyes) in Greek mythology.

5: Amphitrite, the wife of the sea-god Poseidon, is herself associated with the sea. In Ronsard's metaphor, if the sun is still in the ocean, the day has not yet dawned.

III

Donne moy tes presens en ces jours que la Brume
Fait les plus courts de l'an, ou de ton rameau teint
Dans le ruisseau d'Oubly dessus mon front espreint,
Endor mes pauvres yeux, mes gouttes et mon rhume.

Misericorde ô Dieu, ô Dieu ne me consume
À faulte de dormir, plustost sois-je contreint
De me voir par la peste ou par la fievre esteint,
Qui mon sang deseché dans mes veines allume.

Heureux, cent fois heureux animaux qui dormez
Demy an en voz trous, soubs la terre enfermez,
Sans manger du pavot, qui tous les sens assomme:

J'en ay mangé, j'ay beu de son just oublieux,
En salade cuit, cru, et toutesfois le somme
Ne vient par sa froideur s'asseoir dessus mes yeux.

III

In these days of winter when daylight wanes,
Grant me your gifts, or else from your bough
That's been dipped in the Lethe, besprinkle my brow:
Let my poor eyes sleep, and my nose, which constantly drains.

Have mercy, O Lord! Do not inflict the pains
Of sleeplessness on me. I'd rather now
By plague or by some fever be laid low,
Which my dried-up blood fires in my veins.

Happy those beasts that sleep so gently lulls
For half the year within their earthen homes,
Not eating poppy, which overwhelms and dulls.

I've eaten and drunk of its forgetfulness
In salads, cooked or raw, but nonetheless
Upon my eyes sleep's numbness never comes.[3]

---

3. The translation varies between anapestic tetrameter and iambic pentameter.

Line 3: The river of forgetfulness ("le ruisseau d'Oubly"), one of the rivers of the Underworld in Greek mythology, is Lethe. Ronsard's phrase corresponds to the forgetfulness ("oublieux") associated with poppy in lines 11-14.

IV

Ah longues nuicts d'hyver, de ma vie bourrelles,
Donnez moy patience, et me laissez dormir,
Vostre nom seulement, et suer et fremir
Me fait par tout le corps, tant vous m'este cruelles.

Le sommeil tant soit peu n'esvente de ses ailes
Mes yeux tousjours ouvers, et ne puis affermir
Paupiere sur paupiere, et ne fait que gemir,
Souffrant comme Ixion des peines eternelles.

Vieille umbre de la terre ainçois l'umbre d'enfer,
Tu m'as ouvert les yeux d'une chaisne de fer,
Me consumant au lict, navré de mille pointes:

Pour chasser mes douleurs ameine moy la mort.
Hà mort, le port commun, des hommes le confort,
Viens enterrer mes maux, je t'en prie à mains jointes!

IV

Ah, long winter nights that torture me,
Grant me a respite; let me sleep and forget.
The mere thought of you makes my body sweat
And shake all over: such is your cruelty.

Sleep's wings do not fan—in the slightest degree—
My eyes; always open, they cannot set
Eyelid on eyelid: I can only fret,
Suffering like Ixion eternal agony.

Old shadow of the earth—or of hell, I should say,
You keep my eyes open with an iron chain,
Consuming and wounding me in every way:

Bring death to me now to drive away pain.
Ah, death, common harbor and comfort of men,
Come, bury my afflictions—with clasped hands I pray![4]

---

4. The translation varies between iambic and anapestic measures.

Line 9: Night (the Greek *Nux*) in Hesiod's *Theogony* is born from Chasm (the meaning of the Greek *Chaos*) and gives birth to Death (*Thanatos*). In Hesiod, Night has its home in *Tartaros* (one of the names for the Underworld.

V

Quoy mon ame, dors tu engourdie en ta masse?
La trompette a sonné, serre bagage, et va
Le chemin deserté que Jesuchrist trouva,
Quand tout mouillé de sang racheta nostre race.

C'est un chemin facheux borné de peu d'espace,
Tracé de peu de gens que la ronce pava,
Où le chardon poignant ses testes esleva,
Pren courage pourtant, et ne quitte la place.

N'appose point la main à la mansine, apres
Pour ficher ta charue au milieu des guerets,
Retournant coup sur coup en arriere ta vue:

Il me faut commencer, ou du tout s'emploier,
Il ne faut point mener, puis laisser la charue,
Qui laisse son mestier, n'est digne du loier.

V

Soul, why do you sleep in your body's dull mass?
The trumpet has sounded, so pack up and go.
Take a path that's deserted, which Christ led us to,
When, soaked in his blood, he redeemed our whole race.

It's a path paved by brambles, so narrow in space
That few men have traced it (it's one they eschew);
For piercing thorns raise their heads when they do.
But gather your courage: don't yield up your place.

Do not set your hand to the shaft for the sake
Of driving your plough through the midst of a furrow
With stroke upon stroke, while still looking back.

When once one begins, one has to be thorough.
There's no point in leaving the plough one has driven:
Who abandons his craft isn't worthy to have striven.[5]

---

5. The translation is in anapestic tetrameter.

Line 2: The apocalyptic sounding of the trumpet occurs in the New Testament Book of Revelation.

8: "[N]e quitte la place" in French, which I translate in a perhaps overly literal way here, has the meaning of "Don't abandon your endeavor."

9-14: In Ronsard's strangely convoluted conception in this sonnet, driving a plough seems metaphorically associated with the poetic process (and with the courage to pursue it to the end); but as the octave urges the soul to follow the path discovered by Christ, there seems also to be a connection between holiness and poetry.

VI

Il faut laisser maisons et vergers et Jardins,
Vaisselles et vaisseaux que l'artisan burine,
Et chanter son obseque en la façon du Cygne,
Qui chante son trespas sur les bors Mæandrins.

C'est fait j'ay devidé le cours de mes destins,
J'ay vescu j'ay rendu mon nom assez insigne,
Ma plume vole au ciel pour estre quelque signe
Loin des appas mondains qui trompent les plus fins.

Heureux qui ne fut onc, plus heureux qui retourne
En rien comme il estoit, plus heureux qui sejourne
D'homme fait nouvel ange aupres de Jesuchrist,

Laissant pourrir ça bas sa despouille de boue,
Dont le sort, la fortune, et le destin se joue,
Franc des liens du corps pour n'estre qu'un esprit.

VI

Our dwellings and our orchards and our gardens we must leave,
The vessels and the vases that our artisans engrave,
And chant our funeral dirges, as the Swan with his last breath
Does upon Maeander's shores to celebrate his death.

I have unwound my destiny's allotted thread—it's done.
I've made my name significant: I've lived and I am known.
My pen flies upward to the sky, there to become a sign—
Far from the worldly snares to which even the wise incline.

Happy is he who never was; more happy, who returns
Back to the void from whence he came; more happy who sojourns
With Jesus Christ, an angel now, though human formerly,

Leaving to putrefy on earth his cast-off body's clay
(With which fate, hazard, destiny, fortune, and chance all play)
To be pure spirit—from the body's heavy chains set free.[6]

---

6. The translation is in "fourteeners"—iambic heptameter. For a discussion of this poem, see the Introduction.

Lines 3-4: The swan is reputed to sing when it is about to die. Ronsard refers to the Maeander River in Sonnet XLIX of *The Second Book of Sonnets for Hélène* above.

5: The three Fates (*Moirai* in Greek, *Parcae* in Roman mythology), Clotho, Lachesis, and Atropos, were said respectively to spin, measure, and cut the thread of life. The individual soul was therefore less of an actor than an acted-upon entity. But note that Ronsard claims to have unwound his destiny's allotted thread of his own accord.

6: "Insigne," the rhyming word in the French, which I have rendered as "significant," means "famous," "renowned," or "recognized."

7: "Plume" in the French can mean both "pen" (as I have rendered it) and "feather"; thus the word refers back to the Swan of line 3 and at the same time is a metonymy for poetry. At the same time, "signe" ("sign"), the rhyming word, is a homophone for "Cygne." Thus, Ronsard's poetry flies upward to the heavens where it becomes part of the Swan constellation, Cygnus.

9-14: The ancients believed that "Never to have lived is best," as the Chorus says in Sophocles's *Oedipus at Colonus* (in Yeats's translation). But here a pagan pessimism, which sometimes sees the soul as emerging out of and returning to nothingness ("qui retourne / En rien comme il estoit"), is joined to a Christian-Platonist eschatology.

About the Translator

A native of Montreal, Henry Weinfield received a BA from the City College of New York, where he edited the award-winning poetry journal *Promethean*, and a PhD from the Graduate Center of the City University of New York. His verse translations include versions of the *Collected Poems* of Stéphane Mallarmé (University of California Press, 1994; paperback 1996), Hesiod's *Theogony and Works and Days*, done in collaboration with Catherine Schlegel (University of Michigan Press, 2006), and *The Chimeras* by Gérard de Nerval (Dos Madres Press, 2019). His translations of Mallarmé are included in T*he Norton Anthology of World Masterpieces*, 7th ed. vol. 2. In addition, he is the author of three literary studies: *The Poet without a Name: Gray's Elegy and the Problem of History* (Southern Illinois UP, 1991), *The Music of Thought in the Poetry of George Oppen and William Bronk* (Iowa UP, 2009), and *The Blank-Verse Tradition from Milton to Stevens: Freethinking and the Crisis of Modernity* (Cambridge UP, 2012). His most recent collection of poetry is *As the Crow Flies* (Dos Madres Press, 2021). He is the editor of William Bronk's *Selected Poems* (New Directions, 1995) and *From the Vast and Versal Lexicon: Selected Poems of Allen Mandelbaum* (Pennyroyal Press, 2018). In 2018 he received a fellowship from the National Endowment for the Arts to complete the translation of Ronsard contained in this volume. Weinfield is Professor Emeritus of Liberal Studies and English at the University of Notre Dame, where he taught from 1991 to 2019. He lives in New York City.

Photograph of the translator by Lois Greenfield. Used by permission.

www.ingramcontent.com/pod-product-compliance
Lightning Source LLC
Chambersburg PA
CBHW021854230426
43671CB00006B/382